R.E.I. Editions

All of our ebooks can be read on the following devices:
- Computer
- eReaders
- iOS
- android
- Blackberries
- windows
- Tablet
- Cellular

Daphne & Chloé

Bach Flowers

ISBN: 978-2-37297-1300

Published: November 2014
New updated edition: January 2023

Daphne & Chloé

Bach Flowers

REI Editions

Book Index

Bach Flowers

Bach flowers - or Bach flower remedies - are an alternative medicine created by the British doctor Edward Bach, born on 24 September 1886 in Moseley from a Welsh family in England. He graduated in medicine in 1912 and immediately worked in the emergency room of the university hospital where he began to be noticed for the large amount of time he devoted to patients. He was quick to criticize other doctors for studying the disease as if it were separate from the individual, without focusing on the patients themselves. He became a leading pathologist and bacteriologist.

He discovered that some chronic diseases were caused by intestinal bacteria that until then had not been given due importance. Thus he created some vaccines that gave surprising results on many ailments. In 1917 he was struck by a very serious illness and they promised him a few months to live. Since then he worked tirelessly to fulfill his dream of finding a truly simple, harmless and effective therapy. From 1919 to 1922 he worked at the homeopathic hospital in London, but he was not satisfied with homeopathy, his criticism was moved by the belief that toxic and poisonous substances could not have a real healing function. He collected countless plant samples, but nothing gave a clear answer, until he prepared Impatiens, Mimulus and Clematis with the homeopathic method, finally obtaining results. It was these flowers that encouraged him to leave the city and move to Wales to devote himself fully to his research. On a May day she realized that the dewdrops placed on the flowers were magnetized by the energy of the morning sun, a more powerful and natural dynamization than the sequence used in homeopathy; thus the new method was born.

- From 1930 to 1936 he made his books and his 38 remedies.

His passion brought him into conflict with the medical board who struck him off the register the same year he died, having exhausted his strength in the grueling search for his remedies.

He died convinced that he had finished his work on November 27, 1936, leaving us an extraordinary legacy: a new healing technique.

It is well known that our emotional states have a profound influence on our well-being and health.

An altered emotional state that repeats itself every day creates real dysfunctions in our body; 90% of the causes of man's disease come from planes beyond the physical, and it is on these planes that symptoms begin to manifest before the physical body shows any disturbance.

- Bach Flowers rebalance emotions and address only and exclusively how we react emotionally to the vicissitudes, experiences and problems in our days. Bach flower essences have the quality and ability to change a negative emotion into a positive one; for example, a person with low self-esteem, after taking specific floral essences, will begin to believe in herself again and day by day she will be more self-confident. Negative emotions are not suppressed, but transformed into the opposite positive emotional state, for example fear of failure in self-confidence or impatience in calmness and tranquility. They can therefore be useful in the face of an illness, not from a physical point of view but just as a mood support.

The person is seen as a complete individual where emotions are a pivotal point, and not just as a physical body with symptoms; it is therefore necessary to analyze the emotional state and not the physical symptoms, on the basis of which the suitable remedies are found. In fact, subjects with identical physical problems react and live with different emotions and feelings. Bach Flowers do not help to repress negative attitudes, but transform them into their positive side and can be used in cases of: anxiety, ambition, perfectionism, joint pain, addiction to alcohol, drugs, smoking, insomnia, indecision, uncertainty, influenceability, hypochondria, mourning, abandonment, separation, illness, convalescence, skin, teeth, guilt, sexuality, stress, menopause, pregnancy, elderly, depression, melancholy, loneliness, shyness, insecurity, travel (nausea vomiting), school exams , possessiveness, jealousy and to protect oneself from the influences of others (useful in professions such as doctors, nurses, therapists).

- Bach flowers have no contraindications and do not interact with medicines; they are 100% natural and can be used successfully by children and adults. They are completely safe and harmless, there are no side effects, overdose is not possible and they are not addictive. Finally, they can be used without interference in combination with other medicines and/or other forms of treatment, including homeopathy.

Bach flower essences can be applied in many areas, they affect all aspects of psychological and emotional health. There are 38 different Bach flower essences, and each acts on a specific emotional state. Most of the time up to seven different essences are mixed in one bottle to directly address a specific problem. Bach has thus divided the 38 flowers from which the remedies are drawn.

- The very first flowers discovered by Bach were the so-called "12 Healers", which the Welsh doctor began to experiment first on himself and then on his patients; the other 26 were discovered a short time later, divided into "7 Helpers" and "19 Assistants".

Bach advised to pick the flowers in the period of maximum flowering and in the early hours of the morning of a sunny day, with no clouds in the sky; the intact flower was placed in a bowl of spring water in the field where it had been picked and was treated according to the sun method. The other method, known as boiling, consisted in boiling the buds or buds on their own twigs. These are the only two methods of preparation reported in the works of the Welsh physician.

- **Sun method**

The sun method is very simple. Meanwhile, it is necessary to work on a hot and sunny day, obviously in the period of maximum flowering of the plant.

The flowers must be collected on the spot, without being touched with the hands, and cutting them with scissors, the buds are dropped into a 300 ml fine glass container, filled with pure water, taking care to cover the surface of the basin with them . Then they are left to macerate in the sun for 4 hours (in Italy, where the sun is hotter than in Wales, 3 is enough); in this way the sun would transfer the flower's vibration to the water below. At the end of this period, the water of the flowers is filtered with a paper filter in a 1-litre bottle, adding an equal dose of cognac (or brandy), which is used for conservation.

The liquid obtained is called mother tincture of Bach flowers. As for Rock Water, the procedure is different. In fact, since it is simple water from an ancient English spring known for its healing properties, it is enough to collect this water in the usual container (without touching it with your hands), leave it for four hours in the sun and then dilute it with brandy, as first described.

The 20 remedies are prepared with the sun method: Oak, Gorse, White Chestnut, Water Violet, Mimulus, Agrimony, Rock Rose, Centaury, Scleranthus, Wild Oat, Impatiens, Chicory, Clematis, Vervain, Heather, Cerato, Gentian, Olive , Vine and Rock Water.

- **Boiling method**

The boiling method is faster. Once the young flower shoots have been collected with the same method, they will have to be placed in a porcelain metal pot, approximately in the same quantity as in the first method but with a liter and a half of water. Left to boil for about 30 minutes, the tincture thus obtained will be left to cool, then adding the same quantity of brandy to the filtered water. The 18 remedies are prepared with the boiling method: Aspen, Elm, Cherry Plum, Beech, Chestnut Bud, Crab Apple, Holly, Honeysuckle, Hornbeam, Star of Bethlehem, Sweet Chestnut, Walnut, Wild Rose, Willow, Pine, Mustard, Larch, Red Chestnut.

Here are some rules and news relating to Bach flowers:

- The small bottle of the mix can contain a maximum of seven Flowers, this is because otherwise the effectiveness of the single Flowers would decrease considerably.
- Bach Flowers are a simple and natural treatment, they are absolutely not harmful and have no contraindications of any kind. They can be used for newborns from day one and for the elderly of any age. They are good for animals and help your plants grow strong and robust.
- Bach flowers do not cause any interaction with medicines, whether they are allopathic medicines or homeopathic remedies.

They have no biochemical effect, it is not necessary to stop taking the Flowers if you get sick or have to start a treatment, you can continue taking the contraceptive pill or pressure pills or any medicine your doctor has prescribed. In fact, the preparation of the Mother Tincture of Flowers takes place without the use of parts of the plant or flower that could cause allergic states, in Bach Flowers there is no presence of pollen, Bach Flowers cannot be combined with any other plant that can commonly cause allergies. If we can identify the negative moods that crop up when we get sick, we can fight the disease better and heal faster. Dr. Bach had come to the conclusion that those who normally use Bach flowers get sick much less. Using floral remedies, we try to influence the deeper structures from which the disease originates.

- Bach remedies can be found on the market in herbalists and pharmacies.
- For the assumption, take 2 drops of pure remedy for each Flower chosen and mix with 3-4 drops of water and 1/4 of Brandy. In practice, it is sufficient to fill the glass bottle up to a finger from the brim with natural water and add a teaspoon of Brandy, in this way we will have the right conservation of our mix.
- We can distinguish two types of preparations:
    - ✓ The stock bottle, bottle containing 7.5 or 10 ml of the pure remedy.

- ✓ The ready-to-use 30 ml bottle, where the remedies you want to take are added to a base of water and brandy.
- The mixture with Bach flowers must always be kept in the dark, as light produces photochemical phenomena which alter the extracts of any type of medicinal plant.
- The bottle of the Flower mixture should never be kept in the refrigerator, because it would be immersed in an electromagnetic field, furthermore the Bach Flowers, being obtained with the sun and boiling method, would undergo an alteration of their action due to the cold.
- Bach Flowers do not create any type of addiction, they have no side effects and can be taken with complete peace of mind by anyone, they have no contraindications, they do not create side effects or addiction, nor addiction, nor unpleasant interactions with medicines or other preparations or substances.
- Despite being a great help and support, they never replace medical therapy, therefore, for physical problems, always contact your doctor.
- It is important to remember that the remedies contain a small amount of brandy as a preservative. For alcoholics or for those who have problems with alcohol, it is advisable to contact their doctor, or for religious reasons to competent people they trust. It is also possible to put the remedies in hot liquids in order to completely evaporate the alcohol.

Dr Bach later abandoned the distinction between 'Healers', 'Helpers' and 'Assistants' as superfluous, but many people around the world still use it.

The 12 Healers :

- Agrimony, for those who hide their torments behind a cheerful and courteous façade.
- Centaury, for those with a lack of will, who are easily influenced or overly altruistic.

- Chicory, for those who love possessively, trying to do everything possible to be reciprocated.
- Rock Rose, for those in great fear and panic.
- Gentian, for those who indulge in pessimism, get discouraged and easily depressed.
- Mimulus, for those with fear or anxiety of unknown origin.
- Impatiens, for those who are impatient and cannot tolerate interference with their rhythms.
- Cerato, for those who lack self-confidence and continually seek advice from others.
- Scleranthus, for those undecided between two choices.
- Vervain, for those who get too carried away by enthusiasm and have a strong sense of justice.
- Water Violet, for those who like to be alone and are sometimes proud.
- Clematis, for those who daydream, living more in the future than in reality.

The 7 Helps :

- Rock Water, for those who are very rigid in their way of being and want to set an example.
- Wild Oat, for those unsure of their role in life.
- Heather, for those who don't like being alone and often strike up conversations, just to be able to talk to others and who are self-centered.
- Gorse, for those in great despair and feeling stuck.
- Olives, for those who are exhausted due to physical or mental fatigue.
- Oak, for those who can't disconnect, works hard and never gives up.
- Vine, for those who feel the desire to dominate others.

The 19 Assistants :

- Holly experiences anger, envy and hatred, strong negative feelings towards others.

- Honeysuckle, for those who miss the past or who are homesick.
- Hornbeam, for those who can't start the day with the right energy.
- White Chestnut, for those who have constant and unwanted thoughts, and want peace of mind.
- Sweet Chestnut, for those experiencing extreme anxiety, where nothing but destruction is seen.
- Red Chestnut, for those who feel apprehension for their loved ones.
- Beech, for those who want to see more beauty and are sometimes intolerant of others and critical of them.
- Chestnut Bud, for those who always repeat the same mistakes.
- Larch, for those who have low self-esteem, and are afraid of failing.
- Crab Apple, for those who need cleansing in body or mind.
- Cherry Plum, for those afraid of losing reason and self-control.
- Walnut, for those who have to face major changes and need protection from external influences.
- Elm, for those who feel overwhelmed with responsibility.
- Pine, for those with a strong sense of guilt.
- Aspen, for those who are afraid of vague, indistinct things for no apparent reason.
- Wild Rose, for those who abandon themselves to resignation and apathy.
- Willow, for those who feel bitterness and resentment.
- Mustard, for those who feel momentarily unhappy and cannot say why.
- Star of Bethlehem, for those who have suffered an emotional shock.

The seven groups of Flowers

The field on which the Bach Flowers act the most is that of emotion and moods, but certainly, as psychosomatic medicine teaches, the mind is not detached from the body, and what is shown on a mental level has a meaning and an influence also on the physical plane.

The signals that the emotions give are only signals preceding those of the body, i.e. the physical symptoms, therefore by observing and knowing the emotional and mental aspect it is also possible to correct what happens in the body.

According to Bach, the human being can fall into seven fundamental traps which place him in antagonism, rather than in harmony, with himself, with the other, with Creation. These are psychological traps, positions and mental rigidities that prevent the ego from taking its right boundaries, thus allowing it to invade and block the development of the soul. These basic negative attitudes are fear, uncertainty, disinterest in the present, loneliness, excessive suggestibility, despondency or hopelessness, and the desire to direct the lives of others.

- They all have in common an unbalanced ego: hypertrophied, too centered on himself and, therefore, not very sensitive to the needs of the other, or, on the contrary, convoluted, incapable of affirmation and not very sensitive to the needs of the individual himself.

To each group belong certain flowers, which share the basic negative trait that underlies them. Flower therapy does not cure the disease, but people's moods and reactions to events.

For example: how do we react to a certain event? With anger, fear, indifference, discouragement?

The response we give to the event or symptom tells us which flowers will be useful to us at that moment.

Bach therefore divided the 38 flowers he discovered for their healing virtues into seven distinct groups.

- 1st group: for fear
- 2nd group: for those who suffer from uncertainty

- 3rd group: due to insufficient interest in the present
- 4th group: for solitude
- 5th group: for hypersensitivity to influences and ideas
- 6th group: for discouragement or despair
- 7th group: for excessive worry

1st group: for fear

The first group of flowers is what Bach himself listed first, the remedies for fear:
- Aspen - assistants
- Mimulus - Healers
- Red Chestnut - Assistants
- Cherry Plum - Assistants
- Rock Rose - Healers

In fear, the ego was unable to assert itself and therefore did not become aware of its strength. And it cannot thus give support to the individual. The person perceives himself too fragile to face trials and pain, while tending to see others and the environment as more powerful than they really are. She withdraws into herself, basically closed and defensive, preventing herself from growing.

Each of the flowers in this first group has its own particular characteristic:
- Mimulus differs from Aspen, because the first concerns specific and precise fears (for example animals, public speaking), the second those indefinite (for example, the dark).
- Red Chestnut is the flower for those who are afraid that something will happen to their loved ones.
- Cherry Plum is the flower for those who fear losing control in times of crisis
- Rock Rose is the panic flower, for when you feel like you're stuck and can't be ready and clear-headed.

Obviously this is a very schematic distinction, it must then be traced back to the individual moments of life, for example, a parent who easily loses patience with their children could benefit from Cherry Plum, because in that moment they are losing control. It is always appropriate to use flexibility and intuition to associate flowers with moods.

2nd group: for the uncertainty

In uncertainty, the Ego has not structured its own scale of values and opinions, and it still perceives itself incomplete in order to be able to accept the responsibilities of the choices, including those that determine which place it will occupy in the world. There is a basic rigidity, ego, for which the person does not accept to risk and prefers to remain stationary in no man's land. Behind the uncertainty hides the fear of making a mistake or that of being diminished as people in case of losing things. If the multiplicity of possible choices that present themselves in life creates a crisis, then this is the case with Wild Oat, while if uncertainty arises only when one is faced with a choice between two possibilities, then one happily resorts to Scleranthus, the flower for those who find themselves teetering between two alternatives. If you feel the need to receive advice on what to choose, even though you already know that you will easily do without your opinion, then you can opt for the beautiful Cerato flower.

In this group Bach also placed three other flowers which, apparently, might seem less relevant: Gorse, Gentian and Hornbeam.

In this second group Bach inserts:

- Cerato - Healers
- Scleranthus - Healers
- Gentian - Healers
- Gorse - Help
- Hornbeam - Assistants
- Wild Oat - Help

The latter often shows his uncertainty in the morning, when, despite restful sleep, there is a feeling that something is still not working well, then starting to move it passes. Gentian, on the other hand, is the flower for those who tend to give up when faced with a small obstacle.

Uncertainty shows itself in the lack of security in the face of what represents an unexpected event, considering it only an obstacle instead of a moment for reflection and improvement. Gorse is a magnificent flower that helps in all those moments in which the spirit feels empty and without solutions, but that despite this, continues to hope for the solutions that others offer it. The energy level in this case is very low, but Gorse is really powerful and immediately restarts his strength.

3rd group: due to insufficient interest

The lack of interest in the present is often the result of a rigidly passive attitude, whereby the person is not interested in what he does not like or which requires an effort to adapt. He doesn't accept the game that life offers to play because he would like only his own rules to apply. Behind it often hides the desire for exceptionality and the fear of having none at all. When despite being in a place or situation, you are not involved, it is appropriate to think of this group of flowers that Bach developed precisely to bring attention back to the "here and now". You can escape from a situation for various reasons, and with different methods. In the Bach Flowers the interest is focused on "how" one flees instead of "why" one flees. Bach Flowers are not chosen for the "symptom" or "situation", but on the basis of the emotional response that the person implements.
In this third group Bach inserts:
- Clematis - healers
- Honeysuckle - Assistants
- Wild Rose - Assistants
- Olives - help
- White Chestnut - Assistants
- Mustard - assistants
- Chestnut Bud - Assistants

It is so evident how important it is to approach flower therapy in an open and prejudice-free manner. Above all, it is advisable to open your heart and mind to emotions, with the certainty that only a full acceptance of the value of emotions allows you to transform them thus living a fully happy and joyful life. Fleeing from reality and taking refuge in the future, in the abstractions of what one would like to do, it is appropriate to consider Clematis, the flower for those who have a fervent fantasy and imagination and who are unable to make their characteristics concrete; it is the flower par excellence that facilitates concentration. If instead of the present one takes refuge in the past, in memories, in the nostalgia of what happened, and that one would still like to see repeated, by choosing Honeysuckle, one will allow the harmonious detachment from the constraints of the past by accepting the beauty of growing up today. When daily reality, with all its little routines, becomes heavy and uninteresting, and you begin to feel listless, little interested in what you live, always looking for something different from the "usual", choose the strength of Wild Rose, the flower that allows you to see the beauty and creative strength even in the little things of every day, creating interest in life. For lack of energy, when one is completely exhausted, perhaps after an event in which one gave all one could give, one resorts to the energy of Olive, the flower of the olive tree.

- This plant represents resilience well. Observe how strongly the olive tree recovers after frosts or after radical pruning.

Both in Wild Rose and in Olive one is tired, the difference consists in the fact that in the first case it is sufficient to do something different to feel good, while in the second, there is no difference, the tiredness is more physical and remains in spite of everything .

There are two other ways to escape from reality, one when the mind is busy thinking and rethinking about something fixed, the other when, instead, through drastic mood changes, one is unable to be present in everyday experiences.

In the first case the corresponding flower is White Chestnut, also known as the remedy for the "striped disc", precisely because the mind always keeps turning on the same point, just like a damaged disc.

The second relates to the state that Mustard can cure, in other words to those sudden situations where everything is suddenly black and just as quickly returns to normal. The reason for neither sadness nor happiness is known. The last flower of this group is suitable for all those situations in which one always falls into the same mistake, the child who studies and always makes mistakes on the same point, the adult who claims that he always falls in love with the wrong person. In this case one remains connected to the past without experiencing it.

- Chestnut Bud is the flower that allows you to learn from any situation. For this reason Chestnut Bud and Clematis are part of a mixture that is particularly useful for anyone who studies and cannot concentrate sufficiently.

Along with these two flowers are also found: Gentian, Larch and Elm. Specific flowers can also be added to this recipe for exams, now consolidated at an international level; if you are afraid, if you are in a hurry.

4th group: for solitude

A wrong relationship with loneliness, where this borders on isolation, or, on the contrary, is absolutely not tolerated, implies a lack of autonomy, or a fundamental distorted relationship with others, who are never seen and accepted for what they are , but always in relation to the pleasure or disturbance they can cause. Behind loneliness there is the fear of losing the limits of one's ego, which is perceived as fragile, in intimacy and in relationships. And often selfishness, whereby one does not want to concern oneself with anyone. On the other hand, the inability to be alone reveals a lack of growth of the ego, so that the person can be completed only through others. Often the anguish that occurs in loneliness also denounces a bad relationship with oneself. In this journey within oneself, to discover emotions and one's personal response to situations, one certainly encounters an emotion known to many: loneliness. Among the Bach flowers, there are only three flowers that harmonize the feeling of solitude: Impatiens, Water Violet and Heather. Three very different ways of feeling alone, three ways of understanding how everyone is responsible for this loneliness.
In this fourth group Bach inserts:
- Water Violet - Healers
- Impatiens - Healers
- Heather - Help

Through the use of flowers one can change the response to surrounding situations and change the feeling of loneliness into Love.
How do these three flowers differ?
In Water Violet we meet wise but detached people who prefer a quiet life in their own home, in their own environment. They don't like mixing with others, although they are much sought after by others for their wise advice. Water Violet types tend to be as strong on the outside as they are actually fragile on the inside. They well represent the image of this flower growing in water in shady places, its delicate stem is at the same time rigid,

as symbolically as Water Violet people are in life. They are not cold in relationships but certainly detached, often due to their original ideas.

Their loneliness is due precisely to this choice of quiet of theirs, they can easily be confused with Mimulus people, but the latter shun others out of fear, while Water Violets out of detachment.

Impatiens corresponds to the person who is alone because his rhythms are fast, and believes that others do not correspond to his own. According to the Impatiens types, the others are all too slow, they don't immediately understand what is being said to them, they don't leave as soon as the traffic light is green. Suffice it to say that this flower is so called precisely because, when the seed is ripe, it is sufficient for the plant to be touched to be immediately spat out. Impatiens is also called "do not touch me" and corresponds perfectly to the person who wakes up in the morning and does not want to be disturbed by anyone in any way. The positive aspect of Impatiens allows these people to be able to accept the rhythms of others, thus being able to be close to others.

Heather people are defined as needy children who, in order to be the center of attention and not to go unnoticed, will strike up a conversation with anyone and about anything. Their interest is directed only to themselves.

Maybe they ask how the others are doing, but as soon as the question is finished and without waiting for any answer, they immediately start talking about their latest "misfortune" and never stop, not even when their interlocutors, by now tired, try to leave.

They are people closed in on themselves, they hardly listen.

Often behind these people we find a difficult childhood where they did not receive answers and attention from the surrounding environment, and now, even if they are grown up, they try in every way to make up for their loneliness by always being close to someone, and at the same time, like a dog chasing its tail, they become more isolated because others cannot stand them.

5th group: for hypersensitivity

Excessive sensitivity to the influences of others denounces an immature ego that does not draw on its own resources but prefers to limit itself to reacting to external solicitations. The person lacks psychic and affective autonomy. Behind it often hides the fear of losing the support of the other, and a rigidity that manifests itself in keeping the inner distances from the people with whom one is involved and/or who suffers. The person actually remains involved and closed in on himself, as in the group of uncertainty. No one can stand in the way of what is really true for oneself. The obstacles for which others often blame themselves, with phrases such as: they didn't allow me, they hindered me, they didn't want to.. actually represent only a part of themselves that still doesn't feel they deserve what they really want from life. By doing so you accept that someone else interferes with your personal choices.
In the fifth group Bach inserts:
- Agrimony - healers
- Centaury - Healers
- Walnut - assistants
- Holly - Assistants

For these people, events or situations represent the part of themselves that doesn't really want to go to 100% of their potential. Agrimony is the flower of the clown, of the one who is always smiling and jovial in the presence of others, even when feelings are completely different inside himself.
The Agrimony person in the face of difficulties minimizes, and somehow prefers to escape. Drugs, alcohol, food or smoking are the classic tools Agrimony uses. These products momentarily induce a sense of happiness and relaxation in him, in reality they only remove the problem, then maybe he wakes up at night with a spasmodic hunger. Agrimony is a particularly useful remedy for allowing one's emotions to come to the surface, allowing them to peel off the mask. Initially this is not easy, but surely it would be more difficult not to do it. After all, those

who find themselves in this situation experience a sort of indefinite anguish.

Centaury status is recognized when you become Mr. YES, the one who always says yes to any other request, even when he doesn't want to. Cinderella's flower, the flower of those who would rather please others than themselves. These people are almost afraid to accept the possibility of being able to decide their own lives. You need Centaury when you need to strengthen your center and decision-making power.

Walnut represents among the Bach flowers, the protector from influences. This flower allows you to "shield" yourself from external influences, strengthening yourself, without feeling at the mercy of circumstances or people. When you are meteoropathic, Walnut helps, but also when you are in a moment of change and you want to detach from the "old", Walnut facilitates this step. Walnut blossom is recommended when children are teething, when going to school for the first time, in adolescence, puberty, changes of residence, practically whenever one changes.

Walnut facilitates and helps in this step.

Holly is jealousy personified, she represents the person who doesn't trust others, thinking that they are making fun of her. They are obsessed with what others may think. Holly is a flower with wonderful and beneficial powers for the jealousy of children to whom a little brother or sister is born. Even if parents are very good at not making their children weigh the arrival of another baby, it can be difficult for a child to understand that the love received up to that moment will not change. Holly in this situation allows you to transform any jealousy into Love. This does not happen only in children but in everyone, when you experience a moment of tension with someone, Holly allows you to soften this tension by experiencing the situation better.

6th group: for discouragement

In despondency, the ego surrendered and declared itself powerless in the face of events and the environment. Often the person prefers to collapse rather than questioning and reviewing and trying to change their inner positions. Behind it often hides an ego too stiff in the defensive. The person demands too much of himself and has no trust in others, because deep down he is afraid of not being able to be loved for who he is. This group of flowers is certainly the most varied among the flowers that belong to it. By reviewing the characteristics of each flower we will see how different the meaning of discouragement and despair is between these essences.
What Bach surely meant by despair and discouragement is that feeling that comes when one has the sensation of not being able to proceed further in life, when the life one lives is not accepted for what it is or for what it teaches.
In the sixth group Bach inserts:
- Larch - Assistants
- Pine - assistants
- Elm - Assistants
- Sweet Chestnut - Assistants
- Star of Bethlehem - Assistants
- Willow - Assistants
- Oak - Help
- Crab Apple - Assistants

Larch, the flower of the Larch, is very suitable for those circumstances in which one thinks that others are better, believing that one does not know how to do anything. Very often it is the flower of teenagers, but also of all those people who focus their attention above all on the goal to be achieved, without concentrating and without getting excited about the path to reach the goal. The truth is that you learn along the way, and the result is only a moment of this journey. Larch helps to gain awareness of the experience by instilling self-confidence.

Two other flowers in this group are related to the feeling of not making it, but in very different ways: Elm and Oak are the flowers in question. The first, Elm, is suitable for all those who feel too busy and think that actually "everything is too much". The second, Oak, is the flower of those who can't take it anymore, but who don't listen to each other and who continue unceasingly in their efforts. Oak is the oak flower, of that plant that stands up to everything, even lightning, without ever bending over, even living for many years, then suddenly breaks for no reason. Oak people often feel bad, or experience discomfort on Saturdays and Sundays, that is when they can relax. In such cases Oak becomes their blessing. A separate chapter should be dedicated to Star of Bethelhem, the flower to overcome trauma, in these cases the person's vital energy is blocked by the shock suffered. It's better to point out that whatever is held responsible for a deep disturbance is a cause of shock, it doesn't necessarily have to be something "big". But if it is sometimes believed that some event or situation is responsible for the current state of "deadlock", consider Star of Bethelhem. This flower will put your life energy and self-healing ability back into motion. Discouragement can also come when you take the blame for everything, or when you blame everything on others instead.

It is preferable to use the word responsibility rather than guilt, but to understand the deep meaning of these two flowers, this term will be used anyway.

The Pine person also takes the blame for others, and often resorts to using the word "sorry." They tend to judge themselves too negatively and critically, the series could have done better... but I haven't done it.

Willow people are the classic "grey, heavy" people who consider their life an unfair and unfair life. They feel that others are undeservedly luckier than they are, and they enjoy this "just" resentment of theirs. They never have responsibility.

In both cases, both with Pine and with Willow, the discouragement occurs due to the lack of a sense of responsibility, or of feeling able to respond to situations in one's life. Crab Apple is the flower that is defined as cleansing, this flower allows you to cleanse the body, mind and spirit of everything that is considered "impure". Crab Apple people can be recognized precisely by their morbid attachment to physical appearance and cleanliness. A pimple is a catastrophe, a glass that isn't perfectly clean is definitely dirty, sex is dirty. With Crab Apple you learn to accept yourself for who you are, cleaning up those limiting thoughts, improperly, and often unconsciously, deemed dirty.

The last flower in this long series is Sweet Chestnut, the flower that allows you to light up your path and your life again when you feel like you're in a tunnel, where everything is now useless, even if you don't. he says, even if he doesn't admit it.

It's a flower that not only gives energy like Oak or Elm, but a flower that gives hope, and uplifts by putting everyone in touch with their own spiritual self and with the meaning of life.

7th group: for excessive worry

Being excessively interested in the lives of others, even to bring them well-being, implies a hypertrophied ego that wants to extend its dominion even beyond itself. The person conceives of others solely as a way of escape, through power, from himself and from his own problems. Behind it hides the fear of inner confrontation with oneself, with one's emotional needs and one's fragility. Rigidity is extreme precisely because it has to defend and mask this fear. We and the others, this is the message of this group of flowers. There are some truly unique characters among these five flowers, they all care about others, and they all know how to solve other people's problems. Everyone applies himself in this titanic effort to change the others, perhaps without realizing that all that one wants to change of the others concerns instead something of oneself. Chicory is the flower of the "Italian mamma", which also suits many Italian fathers. Chicory does everything for others, knows how to help others, is loving and caring. Everything is in order, everything is ready for her beloved. In the seventh group Bach inserts:
- Chicory - Healers
- Vervain - Healers
- Vine - Help
- Beech - Assistants
- Rock Water - Help

It is the parent who does everything for the children, then one day the children grow up and love to make their own life.
Chicory then feels abandoned and recriminates that "after all I've done, look how they treat me". Chicory's love for others is of the type, I give you and you give me; it's not quite the unconditional love we talk about so much.
Hiring Chicory transforms this "love blackmail" into a gesture of free love. And here are two opposing flowers, but similar in their desire to change the others: Vervain and Rock Water. But before explaining how they differ, a few words about this last flower, which flower it is not. Rock Water is actually rock

water, spring water generally defined as curative. It is the only non-flower flower, it serves to soften our rigidities, like water does with rock. Rock Water is recognized because it has high ideals, religious and otherwise, which it does not propose to others, but which it simply implements in its own life with stubborn schematicness and with the intention of being an example to others.

On the contrary, Vervain shares all his enthusiasm with the others, his every opinion, sometimes even fanaticism, becomes the need to convince others. Vervain hates injustice, and every little injustice becomes a crusade.

With Rock Water you soften the strong and hard lines, comparing them with others, with Vervain you learn to manage enthusiasm without being fanatic. Beech is the flower of criticism, when it happens that you don't tolerate something in others, or when you recognize their every little obsession, with annoyance, Beech can increase tolerance. Tolerance is accepting that everyone can express themselves freely.

Beech is very useful in intolerances, even allergic ones. In allergies, in fact, you can't stand something, just like Beech can't stand something in his life.

And finally the big boss: Vine. With him, or with her, one does not argue, one executes. The person who needs Vine recognizes himself because he orders others what to do, he's not like other flowers who maybe worry, no, Vine orders, he knows what needs to be done. Vine is a wonderful flower for all those despot children who rule their homes. Vine in the positive state allows us to relate to others, exploiting our managerial skills for everyone.

Agrimony

It belongs to the category of "Healers" and is the fourth medicinal plant that Edward Bach discovered in 1930.
Agrimony is for all those who are afraid to show their feelings, always smiling, often wear the mask of cheerful people, even when they suffer. They use stimulants when they have problems nagging them. In Agrimony the tension, internal anxiety is not manifested with others. What worries is kept hidden and masked with the desire to laugh at all costs. Sometimes Agrimony-type people use alcohol or stimulants to try to maintain this facade of serenity. They usually dislike loneliness, finding it more difficult to wear this mask when alone with themselves.
On the contrary, they always try to surround themselves with friends, parties and blinding lights, while at night, when they find themselves alone with their thoughts, that mental torture that they had managed to repress so well inexorably comes back to haunt them.
The Agrimony remedy helps people with such a character trait to accept the darker sides of life and of their personality and come to terms with them, so that they become more complete human beings, without losing their sense of humour, but being able to laugh at one's problems to solve them rather than hide them.
  * To prepare the floral remedy, the flowers that have just opened or in bud are picked, before bees or other insects have visited them, and are prepared with the sun method between June and August.

Moods and symptoms related to Agrimony in order of importance:
  * Forced joy
  * Anxiety hidden by joy
  * Anxiety and fear
  * Anxiety for which you eat even at night
  * Tendency to avoid discussions

- Anxiety localized in the chest
- Nervous hunger
- Hidden inner conflicts
- Fear of discussions
- Tightness in the chest
- They bite their nails
- Teeth grinding in sleep

Definition of E. Bach

Jovial, cheerful people, full of good humor who love tranquility and are disturbed by quarrels or contrasts, in order to avoid which they are willing to make great sacrifices. Though generally trouble-ridden, restless and preoccupied in body and spirit, they hide such grievances behind their good humor and pranksterism, and are considered good friends to know.
They often make excessive use of alcohol or drugs, to stimulate and help themselves to carry their crosses lightly.

Aspen

It belongs to the category of "Assistants".
Who needs this flower is a person very sensitive to negative energies, usually transmitted from the outside. Aspen is for all undefined and vague fears; that of the dark, of magic, of monsters. Suitable for all people who have a particular sensitivity. When problems are experienced even before they occur. Very suitable for children's fears. Poplar leaves shake easily, a breath of air is enough for them to move. Thus people who need Aspen are sensitive to their surroundings; bad news, other people's illnesses are perceived as their own.
The floral remedy immediately stops the fantasy generated by fear, calms the person giving them optimism, makes them understand that fear was only the fruit of the mind. Furthermore, if a similar state of mind were to recur in life, he will now be able to understand what to do and therefore be able to simply say: I have to stop listening to or reading negative news.
With Aspen your sensitivity becomes a source of security, you increase your courage.

- To prepare the floral remedy, the flowers are collected with their branch and buds. The boiling method is used, and therefore a pot is filled with many twigs so that the water can cover them.

Aspen-related moods and symptoms in order of importance:
- Fear of the dark
- Fear as anticipation
- Anxiety for anticipation
- Fear of unseen forces, of magic
- Anxiety with unmotivated fears
- Vague and indefinite fear
- Fear of aggression
- Indefinite anxiety
- Sudden anxiety

Definition of E. Bach

Vague fears, unknown, for which no explanation or reason can be given. Yet the patient may be frightened by the feeling that something terrible is about to happen, but doesn't know what. These vague, inexplicable fears can haunt you day and night. Sufferers often feel afraid to tell others about their upset.

Beech

It belongs to the category of "Assistants".
Who needs this flower is an intolerant and hypercritical person, he can't find anything good in his life, moreover he notices flaws in everything and everyone; his observation ability is above the norm finding negativity in everything around him, nothing escapes him; this attitude manifests it more openly in the family sphere, with friends and colleagues.
The person with this disposition will often speak his mind, but in a polite way, he will always find a flaw to fix; gifted with a great sense of observation that she could use in the world of work, she will be trusted for her sincerity. The flower remedy calms the desire to criticize and increases the level of tolerance.
The positive aspect of Beech is well represented in the literary or film critic but also in the analyst or therapist; in this case the Beech person puts his strong analytical and critical characteristics at the service of others. On the negative side, there is only the risk of not accepting anything of the differences of others. With Beech you accept other people's points of view and tastes with ease and understanding. This Flower is also indispensable for people who experience food allergies and intolerances, because it helps them to express their thoughts and therefore not to tolerate everything and everyone. It is also advisable for all those unbearable situations such as excessive heat.

- To prepare the floral remedy, take some twigs of about 15 cm with their flowers and fill a pot ¾ full, then boil for half an hour.

Beech-related moods and symptoms in order of importance:
- Intolerance
- You can easily see the faults of others
- Annoyance about anything
- Prejudice
- You can't stand the no
- Inflexible with others

- Intolerance
- Authoritarianism with intolerance
- Exaggerated anger at the cause
- Intolerance with arrogance
- Excessive attention to detail

Definition of E. Bach

For those who feel the need to see more of the good and beautiful in all that surrounds them and, although much may appear wrong, to have the ability to see the good growing within. Thus they can be more tolerant, forgiving, and understanding of the different ways in which each individual and all things strive to reach their ultimate perfection.

Centaur

It belongs to the category of "Healers" and is the seventh medicinal plant discovered by Dr. Edward Bach.
Centaury is the remedy for people who find it difficult to say no to others. They are good-natured and kind and love to help others. Sometimes, however, unscrupulous people take advantage of it and the individual Centaury finds himself, in spite of himself, a slave to the desires and will of others. The Centaury remedy does not numb the Centaury personality, but rather helps this type of person develop courage and self-determination so as to be able to say enough at the right time and not submit to the wishes and orders of others.
The lack of ability to impose one's own opinions and needs makes one weak, even physically. Often one is a Red Cross nurse and behind this great desire to help others hides one's inability to assert oneself and then complain that one feels exploited.
This state of mind can arise in various situations: towards a child, towards a partner, a parent, or as a weakness towards a vice: such as cigarettes, sweets, food, expensive clothes, luxury cars, drugs, gambling, sex.
The essence helps the will and self-respect, gives energy, allows to be able to affirm one's personality and to have a balanced attitude towards others, gives the ability to give but without being overwhelmed. The new self-determination will restore vitality and zest for life. With Centaury you know your values and your needs. You are capable of integrating with others, but respecting your own uniqueness. The person with this disposition will gain energy, become more determined and will be able to express his opinion when necessary.
In Centaury children we find taciturn, humble characters; they are those who do not create any problems for their parents, the so-called "good children".

- The preparation for the floral remedy follows the sun method, taking care to pick the inflorescences (without touching them) from as many plants as possible and then placing them in a basin of pure water until the surface is covered. Between May and September it has star-shaped flowers with five petals, with a tube-shaped corolla and in pink or red bunches. The harvest takes place from June to August.

Centaury-related moods and symptoms in order of importance:
- You are not able to say no, even to food in cases of nervous hunger
- Need for confirmation from others with excessive availability towards others
- Excess of love that makes you forget your own interests
- Altruism that leads to feeling exploited
- Altruism as self-denial
- Low esteem because you tend to serve others
- Anxiety to please others
- Lack of decision-making power
- Pleasure anxiety
- Fear of discussions
- Exaggerated altruism
- Shyness with little individuality

Definition of E. Bach

Kind, quiet, good people, and extremely eager to serve others. They abuse their strength in this pursuit, and their desire to help others grows to such an extent that they become more servants than willing helpers. Their natural goodness leads them to do more than is necessary and in doing so they may neglect their particular life mission.

Waxed

It belongs to the category of "Healers" and is the eighth plant discovered by Edward Bach.

Who needs this flower is a person who has little faith in what he thinks, constantly asks everyone for advice, for every little thing. The person with this nature is really unbearable because he asks a thousand questions, for example when he goes shopping he asks the grocer what is the best product and his thoughts, this happens everywhere: from the hairdresser, to a seminar, to the university, from the specialist, and if he meets a person on the street he gives him the third degree. Indecision is Cerato's keyword, even if in reality it is a lack of faith in one's intuitions. The search for confirmation in others occurs due to a lack of confidence in one's ability to grasp the essence of things. When faced with making a decision, unlike the Scleranthus type, they have no hesitation or difficulty in deciding. However, later on, they begin to have doubts and no longer feel so sure that they have made the right decision. Thus they begin to ask for opinions and advice from others and end up being absolutely confused.

Cerato is the remedy for people in this state of mind to regain confidence in their judgment, so that they are able to hear their inner voice and rely on their intuition.

- For the preparation of the remedy, with the sun method, the flowers are delicately taken just under the glass, many until there are enough to cover all the water contained in a basin.

Cerato-related moods and symptoms in order of importance:
- Need the advice of others
- Keep asking for advice
- Excessive need for information
- Need the opinion of others
- Fear of making mistakes due to indecision
- Uncertainty that requires the opinion of others
- You don't trust your intuitions

- Lack of esteem even if he has intuition
- Continuous change behind the advice of others

Definition of E. Bach

Those who don't have enough self-confidence to make their own decisions. They constantly seek advice from others and are often misled.

Cherry Plum

It belongs to the category of "Assistants". Edward Bach discovered the properties of Cherry Plum in the spring of 1935. Cherry Plum is one of the remedies of the group that Dr. Bach defined for Fear. The Cherry Plum type fear is very specific and is the fear that you are losing control of yourself and that you might do something horrible, such as harming others or thinking about suicide (in this case, notify your Doctor immediately treating). When you are afraid of losing control of your body and mind, you are impulsive and out of control. You are afraid of harming others. It is about to explode. In the Cherry Plum state you feel like a pressure cooker, or you do things you don't want to do, or you have compulsive attitudes such as: continuous shopping, smoking, drinking. Applying yourself to manual activities certainly relieves the extreme tension you feel. With Cherry Plum you are able to manage your energy with confidence and spontaneity. Every situation is a source of strength and ability. The floral remedy acts immediately in situations of strong agitation, it is instantaneous; blocks the fear of losing control. The person will immediately feel a sense of tranquility and serenity, driving the obsessive thoughts away from the mind.

- To prepare the remedy, the boiling method is used, taking young branches with perfect flowers from different trees, before the leaves sprout.

Moods and Symptoms Related to Cherry Plum in Order of Importance:
- Fear of losing control
- Impulses that you fear you can't control
- Fear of madness
- Nervous breakdown
- Rage with sudden fits
- Feeling of inner pressure
- Tremors
- Anxiety held inside

Definition of E. Bach

Fear of overloading the mind, of losing one's reason, of doing frightening things whose consequences one fears, unwanted things that one knows are wrong, yet assails the thought and impulse to do them.
The typology of this flower is par excellence the shadow that we all have and that comes out suddenly; using it helps fight those moments when you feel on the verge of an inner explosion and are afraid of making rash gestures, uncontrolled impulses and terrifying acts, which you feel are wrong, but which are driven by a strong unconscious input to do them. Cherry Plum is an indicated remedy that can be used as Edward Bach also suggests, under medical supervision, for people who experience serious drives, suicidal instincts and personality disorders.

Chestnut Bud

It belongs to the category of "Assistants".
Those who need this flower take longer than others to learn life's lessons.
The person with this disposition easily gets excited about any novelty or a new project, but almost never completes any idea or desire, always leaving everything unfinished. In fact, he starts a job and gets stuck halfway through and immediately starts another one, this attitude can be seen even in small things, such as books started and never finished, always repeating the same mistakes.
The person with this nature has a strong intuition for projects or for a job of the future. The floral remedy helps the person find the constancy to finish the activities started, strengthens the memory, and also makes them immediately understand the mistake made and not to be repeated. It makes the person more active and willing to listen to advice.
It is a very important flower for students and for school learning and not because it favors memory. With Chestnut Bud every life occasion becomes a source of learning and growth. You are free from old limiting patterns.

- The floral remedy must be prepared when the bracts open and the branch begins to grow, leaving the leaves free to expand. Take branches about 12 cm long with clean shears (only white horse chestnut). Use the boiling method.

Moods and symptoms linked to Chestnut Bud in order of importance:
- Difficulty learning
- Apathy in learning
- Distraction due to disinterest
- Relapse into the same behaviors
- Difficulty learning from experiences
- Compulsivity
- Focus only on your own projects

- Lack of spirit of observation

Definition of E. Bach

For those who don't take full advantage of observation and experience, and take longer than others to learn the lessons of daily life.
While for some one experience is enough, for such people it is necessary to have more, sometimes many more, before learning the lesson. As a result, to their chagrin, they find themselves repeating the same mistake over and over again, when once might have been enough, or by observing others, even that one mistake could have been avoided.

Chicory

It belongs to the category of "Healers" and is the fifth medicinal plant discovered by Edward Bach.

Whoever needs this flower is a person who dedicates his mental and physical strength to the needs of the people he loves, exercising a certain amount of control. Usually the person with this nature is easily recognized because he always has something to fix for the loved one: such as the collar of the shirt, the hair, the make-up, he also gives advice on clothing, on the partner, on friendships, and asks that it be reciprocated , as if it were a job, an assembly line I give to you, you give to me. You love others, but you want to be reciprocated.

Classic interested manipulator character who probably won't easily accept this definition.

But if you often think: after everything I've done, look how he treats me. Then it's time to consider Chicory. The person with this disposition will always think how to improve the life of loved ones, because he wants them to be happy, but the flower remedy will help them understand that everyone has their own destiny to follow and that it is not necessary to manipulate; he will also learn to give love, without expecting anything in return. With Chicory you understand the true qualities of love by giving protection and security to others in complete autonomy. It is prepared with the sun method, and since the flower withers quickly you need to have a basin with water ready.

Chicory related moods and symptoms in order of importance:
- Pride in your home
- Jealousy and possessiveness with those you love
- Possessiveness with a need to manipulate others
- Jealousy with possessiveness
- Easy crying
- Exaggerated love for the house
- Hypochondria to get attention
- Critical meddling in other people's affairs

- Sense of abandonment in parents when children become Depressed from not being loved
- Need recognition
- Greed as greed
- Desire to command with authoritarianism
- Abandonment, for parents who recriminate when their children go their own way
- Need for order in model housewives
- Love as possessiveness towards others

Definition of E. Bach

Those who are attentive to the needs of others. They have a tendency to take excessive care of children, relatives, friends and always find something wrong to fix. They continue to fix what they think is wrong, and they take pleasure in doing so. They would always like to have those they love close by.

Clematis

It belongs to the category of "Healers" and is the third plant discovered by Edward Bach.

Who needs this flower is a person who lives in an imaginary world, full of hopes for a beautiful future, lives in fantasy, almost never in the present, daydreams. He is usually an optimistic person.

When he thinks of a project or an idea, his mind begins to fantasize until he forgets about the passing of time; this mental attitude frequently accompanies him and is above all aimed at thinking about a pleasant future. Clematis has his head in the clouds, lacks memory, is easily distracted. Thought is very often directed to the future, sometimes to escape the present and related problems. Head in the clouds, feeling ditzy, daydreaming too much are all characteristics of this Bach flower whose climbing plant grows very high but with a very deep root which makes it difficult to eradicate. Clematis is also suitable for study and concentration and is part of the blend for exams. The transformed aspect of the flower makes it easier to realize one's dreams like its root. The floral remedy acts immediately in situations of fainting, it is instantaneous, it brings the person immediately back to the present. The person, with this nature, will be much more present, his imagination will be limited to an imminent future. With Clematis dreams come true with ability, imagination and practicality; one is perfectly in touch with one's own creativity. Clematis is precious for those children with concentration problems, due to their being dreamy, rather than an intellectual deficiency and for artists who want to seek inspiration, bringing out their creative potential and exploiting it to the full.

- The sun method is used to prepare the flower remedy, with enough clumps filled with many flowers to cover the water (note whether single or double flowers). Clematis is one of the ingredients of Rescue, where it is used to alleviate the state of confusion and daze that can appear in emergency situations.

Moods and symptoms connected to Clematis in order of importance:

- Lack of concentration due to distraction
- You daydream and are inattentive
- Difficulty learning due to lack of concentration
- Lack of concentration due to inattention
- Inveterate dreamers
- Prone to minor accidents due to distraction
- Poor memory for details
- Apathy with drowsiness

Definition of E. Bach

Those who are dreamers, not fully awake, sleepy and without much interest in life. Silent people, not really happy with their current situation, they live more in the future than in the present, in the hope of happier times in which their ideals can be realised. When they fall ill, they generally do not make great efforts to recover and sometimes they even wish for death, in the hope of better times or perhaps to find a loved one they have lost.

Crab Apple

It belongs to the category of "Assistants".
Whoever needs this flower is a person who believes that he is not completely clean, as if he wants to drive some poison out of his body, an evil that has now been generated, or that he thinks he has. One has the sensation of being dirty, polluted, both physically and psychologically.
Also suitable for all those who do not accept themselves.
It is definitely the flower that has the greatest impact on the external shape, therefore on the skin and on our relationship with the body and appearance. With Crab Apple it's easier to accept yourself for who you are, valuing our positive aspects more without remaining anchored to just the physical aspect. Also useful when obsessed with cleanliness. Given its relationship with the skin, it becomes part of the Rescue Cream. The person with this disposition will accept himself more willingly; the floral remedy helps to alleviate the phobias concerning dirt and contact with things that do not belong to your home environment such as going to public toilets, the fear that you may endanger your health will vanish and you will be able to stay in contact even with apparently unclean people. This flower is also considered as the natural "antibiotic" of Edward Bach's flower therapy, since it can also be used as a useful remedy in the treatment of acne, mycosis, warts, skin conditions in general, including allergies and also as an antidote to headache after abusing food, alcohol (here associating it with Agrimony).
It can be applied in the form of a cream on pimples, blisters, eczema, basically any rash.

- In flower therapy the flower is gathered in tufts together with their small branch using very sharp scissors (shears). The boiling method is used.

Crab Apple related moods and symptoms in order of importance:

- Excessive care of personal cleanliness and house

- There is no self-confidence in physical appearance
- Dirt obsession
- Need to wash constantly
- Hypersensitive to the possibility of contagion
- Fear of contagion and of being contaminated
- Pimples and acne that he doesn't feel comfortable with
- Fear of spoiled food
- Purification and cleaning

Definition of E. Bach

This is the purifying remedy.

For those who feel that there is something unclean about them. Often it is something seemingly insignificant; in other cases it may be a more serious disorder, almost neglected compared to the only thing on which the person focuses his attention.

Both types are anxious to get rid of the one thing that is of the most importance to get rid of the one thing that is of the most importance in the mind that seems essential to them to cure. They get depressed if the cure fails. Being a purifier, this remedy cleans wounds if the patient had reason to think that a poison to be eliminated has penetrated.

Elm

It belongs to the category of "Assistants".
When everything is too much this is Elm. Even if you are strong and capable, you do not momentarily feel that you are not good enough. As if the legs could not hold the weight of that moment. Sometimes tiredness is not a real exhaustion but only a mental approach to the commitments that are considered many and too many and that only the idea of having to face them makes you weaker. In doing so, real energy collapses occur resulting in severe headaches, dizziness, a feeling of dizziness, sweating and in extreme cases panic attacks or fainting occur. Once the energy reserve is finished, therefore, it collapses. Elm is particularly suitable when we feel too pressured by situations or responsibilities and think that there are just too many.
The floral remedy immediately gives energy, restores self-confidence in times of excessive stress, allows you not to let yourself be discouraged by the great goals to be achieved and slows down the pace, avoiding collapse. During therapy, if you use this flower and you feel moments in which you have drops in energy, it simply means that the time has come for a break, so it is useless to insist because Elm will take care of blocking the excessive rhythm.
It is contraindicated for pregnant women, due to its extremely strong function of uterine activity and arterial hypertension.

- To prepare the floral remedy, the branches of about 15 cm with flowers are collected, in sufficient quantity to fill a pot by three quarters which is then boiled for half an hour.

Elm-related moods and symptoms in order of importance:
- Momentary discouragement
- momentary inadequacy
- Perfectionism
- Depression because you think you are not strong enough
- Anxiety of perfection with a tendency to overexertion

- Feeling of failure

Definition of E. Bach

For those who are doing good work, following their calling and hoping to do something important, often for the good of humanity. Sometimes they can go through periods of depression when they feel that the task undertaken is too difficult and beyond the possibilities of a human being.
It is useful to compare the Elm-type state with the Larch-type state: in the former case, people welcome challenges and only later and occasionally question their abilities, while Larch personalities are convinced that they will fail until from the beginning and therefore tend not to make even a slightest attempt.

Gentian

It belongs to the category of "Healers" and is the eleventh plant discovered in 1931 by Edward Bach.

Whoever needs this flower is a pessimistic person, he constantly considers the worst side of everything, he always sees the glass half empty, his point of view is constantly negative even in the most trivial situations, and in his projects he prepares himself every time to the negative so as not to be disappointed so if anything the result has not been achieved, she can always say that she expected it anyway.

We are sad, depressed, every obstacle breaks down and we are tempted to give up. The cause of this sadness is generally known, there is a tendency to always have a sort of mistrust, even towards happiness. Gentian depression is always motivated by an objective or mental situation that momentarily holds back our goals. You don't feel down for no reason but you know what causes doubt or sadness. Gentian allows you to recover by evaluating new roads and new ways to achieve our goals. With Gentian you have faith in what you feel, and in what happens in your life. The person with this nature will change his way of seeing life, he will not lose faith at the first obstacle, pessimism will turn into optimism, it will be noticed above all in the eyes.

- For the floral remedy, the flowers are picked just below the glass and prepared with the sun method in August or September.

Gentian-related moods and symptoms in order of importance:
- Depression of known cause
- Discouragement after difficulty
- Discouragement after a relapse
- Depression after failure
- Relapses with discouragement
- Reactive depression
- Sorry for the delays
- Skepticism

- Pessimism

Definition of E. Bach

For those who are easily discouraged. They may get progressively better in sickness or in their daily affairs, but any slightest delay or obstacle in this progress causes them doubts and soon demoralizes them.

Gorse

It belongs to the "Aid" category.
Whoever needs this flower is a person who experiences prolonged or unexpected suffering.
This state of mind also arises in those who are optimistic, because being a person who always manages to find the positive side of situations and therefore to adapt even to what happens in life that is unpleasant for them, they come to the conclusion that this is how they go the things.
You no longer have the strength to do anything about the problem you have, but then you try something again just because someone else pushes you to move. The desperation present in the blocked state of Gorse is distinguished from other types of despondency because in this case one has not yet let go of one's grip and one tries, even if one tries many ways, to get out of it.
Gorse increases confidence in one's goals and destiny without letting go. With Gorse one has hope in one's destiny.
- The flower remedy is prepared with the sun method in April. Pick flowers in a field with plenty of plants. It is interesting to note that Gorse was inserted by dr. Bach in the group of Remedies for uncertainty and not in the one for despair, as instead in the case of the Sweet Chestnut. This shows that the main problem for people in the Gorse mood is the loss of certainty. Therefore, if you can persuade them to see things in a different light, confidence and hope are renewed in them and they can start moving forward again with greater confidence. The Gorse Remedy helps accomplish all of this.

Gorse-related moods and symptoms in order of importance:
- Resignation with despair
- Feeling of incurability
- Painful resignation
- Depression with resignation
- Loss of hope

- Depressions and disappointment after relapse
- Passivity

Definition of E. Bach

For cases of great desperation. These people have given up on the idea that anything can still be done for them. Under persuasion or to please others, they can undergo various treatments, but at the same time they confidently affirm to those around them that there is very little hope of improvement.

Heather

It belongs to the "Aid" category.
Who needs this flower is a person who always tries to communicate with others even for small things, going in constant search of affection and consolation and it is only in this way that he draws his happiness; but if the contact is broken, for whatever reason, the suffering becomes torture.
The problem is that she's afraid of being alone, so the need for company and to be heard becomes an obsession. Heather needs love, to feel valued. In certain situations of suffering or faced with problems that arise, there is a great need to talk about it with others, but when this need to always have someone close becomes excessive and one cannot be alone, Heather comes to help by concentrating own energies within themselves and also making the relationship with others easier. The person with this nature will never love solitude, he will gladly approach others to exchange a few words but this time he will interrupt the conversation with a positive attitude towards himself. He will always seek attention in the group but without exaggerating and without complaining. Precious flower for those who feel self-centered and hypochondriac, who want to listen more to others, who have so much self-confidence and who feel competent that they never doubt their ability to advise or give support.
With Heather you are able to listen and connect with others. You find values for your life.
- To prepare the floral remedy, take the ears above the mature flowers, from several plants, and place them as quickly as possible on the water (sun method).

Heather-related moods and symptoms in order of importance:
- Talkative with anyone
- Need constant attention
- To get attention we invent diseases
- Loneliness that is always avoided
- Easy crying
- Food as obsession

- Possessiveness towards anyone for fear of loneliness
- Self-pity to get attention
- We talk a lot
- Self pity
- Food obsession
- Bulimia with talkativeness
- Anxiety due to excitement

Definition of E. Bach

Those who are always looking for the company of anyone who might be willing, finding it necessary to discuss their business with others, no matter who they are. They are very unhappy if they have to be alone for any time, be it short or long.

Holly

It belongs to the category of "Assistants".

Whoever needs this flower is a person who gets angry easily, yells, offends and is aggressive, snaps violently at anything and this can happen anywhere: in a bar, restaurant, car, on the street; he always overreacts to the circumstance.

In the ultra negative state, in addition to getting angry easily, he completely loses the light of reason by breaking anything, for example if the computer gives problems it is also capable of destroying it, in short, he lashes out at anything only because he cannot react and when he is wronged by a person throws himself at him like a fury. Holly's "negative" state blocks oneself and sees the outside world only as a source of cheating against ourselves, creating hatred and jealousy.

Holly allows you to relax by opening up with trust towards others. The person with this disposition will be more peaceful, the floral remedy calms and no longer makes one lose the light of reason so easily; turn anger into love.

With Holly you live in love, without tension but with the clarity and understanding necessary to love.

Holly is often thought of as the Anger Fix, but that's not necessarily the case. The Holly remedy is used for anger when it is accompanied by hatred, suspicion, envy or jealousy. In other cases of anger, other remedies are needed, such as Impatiens, when the anger is caused by impatience, Vervain, when it is caused by a sense of injustice, or Chicory when the person is angry because he feels offended and hurt by the anger. ingratitude of others. Holly is especially indicated for those who are visceral, twisted, who consequently experience hepatobiliary disorders, biliary colic, diarrhea or constipation, cystitis or pathologies related to the heart; therefore it is also used in children, for their jealousies between brothers and / or sisters; while in adults it can often be dosed together with Chicory, which feels betrayed and mocked.

- The floral remedy is prepared with the boiling method, using the tops of the branches with both male and female flowers and some new leaves.

Holly-related moods and symptoms in order of importance:
- Morbid jealousy
- Rancor with hatred
- Grudge
- Absence of love towards others
- Manifest envy
- Joy for other people's problems
- Anger with hate
- Vengeance
- Cruelty to others
- Aggression due to jealousy
- Bitterness due to disappointment
- Absence of love that leads to feeling alone
- Expressed anger

Definition of E. Bach

For those who are sometimes assailed by thoughts of jealousy, envy, revenge, suspicion. For the different forms of opposition and frown. They can suffer a lot inwardly, although often there is no real cause to justify such unhappiness.

Honeysuckle

It belongs to the category of "Assistants".
Who needs this flower is a person who lives in good past memories forgetting the present life.
This state of mind can arise from many factors, for example: when one is left by the person one loves, the death of a loved one, the son who marries and leaves home, the elderly person who thinks about the past; ultimately we begin to live in good memories forgetting the present and all that follows. The person takes refuge in thoughts of the good times now spent losing touch with reality, and has a strong tendency to speak only of the good past lived discarding negative experiences.
When we tend to idealize the past and would like everything to be as it once was, recent or distant in time. The transformed aspect of Honeysuckle allows us to fully welcome new things and new people. And the past is only a source of joy for what it has given. Honeysuckle is also useful in cases of mourning. The floral remedy brings the person back to the present and facilitates their adaptation to reality, thus creating a healthy detachment from the past. Of course he will still talk about the good memories but only with the people who shared those moments. With Honeysuckle you are aware of the present, transforming memories into strength and purpose for life.
The Honeysuckle Remedy helps these types of people learn from the past without having to continually relive it, so they can move forward into the present and enjoy today and tomorrow.

- For the flower remedy, gather a bunch of flowers with stems and leaves from various parts of the creeper, and use the boiling method. The flowers are red on the outside and white on the inside, then turn yellow when pollinated during the summer. Only red flowers are chosen for Dr. Edward Bach's flower shop.

Honeysuckle-related moods and symptoms in order of importance:

- Regrets

- Regret with nostalgia
- Nostalgia for things or situations that are left behind
- Lack of concentration because you think about the past
- Trapped in the past
- Melancholy for memories

Definition of E. Bach

For those who live far in the past which was perhaps a time of great happiness or remembrance of a lost friend or unfulfilled ambitions. They do not expect to find another happiness similar to the one already experienced.

Hornbeam

It belongs to the category of "Assistants".
Who needs this flower is a person who has great difficulty getting out of bed in the morning, wakes up already stressed as if he had just finished a run, a big job, and his need is to sleep, but more he stays in bed and the more tired he gets up. Once out of bed, the person has great difficulty getting dressed, washing, and as time goes by, the energy magically returns; this happens because he starts consuming stimulating substances such as coffee, tea, cigarettes, chocolate. With Hornbeam every day is a new beginning and gives vitality and stimuli for growth. You are mentally and physically fresh and lively. The flower remedy helps the person above all in the initial push and to make them feel lighter and more elastic. The person will be able to complete his or her work without breaks due to exhaustion.

- The floral remedy is prepared with the boiling method with the tips of the branches cut for a length of about 12-15 cm, to have both the male and female flowers.

Hornbeam-related moods and symptoms in order of importance:
- Boredom for the newspaper
- Tiredness especially in the morning which then passes
- Monday morning apathy
- Mental tiredness
- Tiredness that fades with the news
- Mental saturation
- Doubt about your own strength
- Excessive study stress
- Indecision due to lack of strength

Definition of E. Bach

For those who feel they do not have sufficient strength, mental or physical, to carry the weight of life placed upon them; daily activities seem too heavy to deal with, although they generally manage to complete their tasks.
For those who believe that some parts of the body or mind need to be strengthened before they can easily do their job.

Impatiens

It belongs to the category of "Healers" and was the second plant discovered by Dr. Edward Bach.
Who needs this flower is an impatient person, speaks quickly, eats quickly, dresses quickly, combs quickly, makes up quickly, works quickly, walks quickly, thinks something and immediately acts. Everything is done in a hurry, moving from one thing to another. Slow people are not tolerated, so much so that one prefers to be alone at one's own pace, rather than following the times of others.
Impatiens people need to learn that speed does not equal frenzy. Another symptom of Impatiens is the intractability upon waking. With Impatiens you live your own pace and that of others with patience and availability. Impatiens concentrate is indicated for those who are easily irritable. Because of the impatience felt, the person thinks he has to do everything right away, and for this he adopts a high speed in his actions, thoughts and even in his way of speaking. Her competence and efficiency lead her to allow herself to be irritated and frustrated by slower colleagues and consequently to prefer to work alone.
Due to her strong sense of independence she hates wasting time and in conversations often finishes the sentences of others for them. They are always anxious characters and are subject to tachycardia, have digestive spasms, psycho-emotional disorders, neck pain, cramps and acidity. It is also noted that this flower also works in hyperkinetic children, giving them calm and relief.

- The floral remedy is prepared with the solar method by skipping the lilac-pink flowers, without touching them with your hands, and covering the surface of the water in the basin.

Impatiens-related moods and symptoms in order of importance:
- Advice and interference cannot be tolerated
- Impatience
- Idealism and impatience

- Hyperactivity for which you are constantly moving
- Annoyance for setbacks
- Stuttering from haste
- Bulimia with exaggerated hunger for which one can become aggressive
- Aggression due to impatience
- Hasty decisions
- Neck tense
- Accidents due to excessive haste
- Stiff neck

Definition of E. Bach

Those who are quick in thought and action and want everything done without hesitation or delay.
When sick they anxiously desire a speedy recovery. They find it difficult to be patient with slow people, considering it a fault and a waste of time, and they go to great lengths to make such people more attentive. Often they prefer to work and think for themselves, to be able to do everything at their own pace.

Larch

It belongs to the category of "Assistants".
Who needs this flower is a person who lacks self-confidence.
This attitude is the starting point of negative emotions such as:
fear, pessimism, lack of will, masked tension, distrust of
thinking; in short, the lack of self-confidence determines one of
these directions in the course of life. Clearly the opposite of
what happens to the fanatic, proud and possessive person.
You admire the abilities of others but without envy. Often the
Larch person owes this fear of not making it, and the tendency
not to even try, to a lack of trust received from their parents or
excessive protection from them. The fear of other people's
judgment is very strong to keep aloof not even attempting
action. The Remedy helps these people to move forward
without thinking about successes or failures, because the more
they are capable of risking and getting involved in life, the
greater the results they get. With Larch you are confident in
your abilities, focusing on the path rather than the result. This
flower is particularly suitable for those sensitive children who
are treated by their parents and/or relatives by belittling or
shaming them in front of everyone. The flower can also be used
for those who always tend to get sick from not facing situations.
There are also examples of patients suffering from tachycardia
and arrhythmia, caused by self-distrust and here Larch is a
panacea. Finally, there are also cases where the administration
of Larch has helped those who have sexual disorders, doubting
their own strength, such as performance anxiety and danger of
failure.

- In flower therapy, twigs of 15 cm are prepared, with male
  and female flowers collected from as many trees as
  possible. The boiling method is used, filling a pot three-
  quarters full of water.

Larch-related moods and symptoms in order of importance:
- Performance anxiety
- Hesitant due to lack of confidence

- Fear of failure
- Fear of failing
- Fear of exposing yourself
- Sense of inferiority
- Surrendering spirit
- Creativity blocked
- Cowardice due to lack of self-confidence
- Fear of the opposite sex

Definition of E. Bach

For those who do not consider themselves as good or capable as those around them, they are convinced that they are failing, that they will never succeed, and so they do not even make an attempt, or do not do it with sufficient conviction.

Mimulus

It belongs to the category of "Healers" and was the first plant discovered by Dr. Edward Bach.

Who needs this flower is a person who sees dangers everywhere, is often anxious, fearful and has a great imagination that does not coincide with reality. This state of mind can arise after many frightening events or as a result of particular situations such as an economic crisis, clearly the person begins to live in apprehension fearing losing the house, the car, the land. Fears in Mimulus are specific and precise.

The strong sensitivity to the surrounding world makes one tremble easily, such as, for example, when one has to speak in public or in any case in any "excessive" situation where there is too much noise, too much light, too many people. This flower should also be administered for particular fears such as: tunnel, bridge, height, darkness, open and closed space, because to all intents and purposes they are certain fears. Mimulus is the remedy to stimulate that calm courage and strength that are hidden in these people, so that they can face the daily trials of life with firmness. Mimulus can suffer from palpitations and panic attacks, asthma and chronic laryngitis, premature ejaculation and impotence for fear of failure. This remedy can be a good help for overly shy and sensitive children, who blush easily and who are always in a corner instead of participating in the game, who are afraid of the dark and the outside. In this case Mimulus is not to be confused with Larch, which is a flower for those who lack self-confidence, although the two remedies can be administered together as the dysfunctions could be part of the same character, one is for fear and the other is for lack of trust. With Mimulus you are sure, and you go towards the world with calm, courage and strength, taking into account your own sensitivity.

- The flowers bloom from June to September and are yellow with numerous red spots. Note the peculiarity of this plant that when a lot of wind blows the flowers protect themselves by closing and then reopening with the sun. In flower therapy it is prepared with the solar method: covering the pure water collected in a basin with wild flowers, which grow spontaneously on the banks of the bodies of water.

Moods and symptoms related to Mimulus in order of importance:
- Fear of the plane
- Shyness caused by fear
- Fear that makes you blush
- Fear for known cause
- Aggression that hides shyness
- Anxiety about school
- Anxiety about a known fear
- Fear of animals
- Stuttering due to fears
- Talkativeness due to nervousness or fears
- Fear of open spaces, agoraphobia
- Being in company causes fatigue
- Anxiety about school
- Fear of animated discussions
- Hypersensitive to cold

Definition of E. Bach

Fear of worldly things, sickness, pain, accidents, poverty; fear of the dark, of being alone, of adverse fortune. The fears of everyday life.
These people bear their fears silently and secretly, they don't speak about them freely to others.

Mustards

It belongs to the category of "Assistants".
Who needs this flower is a person who spends moments of life in melancholy or in total despair for no apparent reason, isolates himself from everyone because it is difficult for him to hide this state of mind.
He usually spends his life very seriously and sometimes he doesn't experience the emotion because he is afraid of suffering, thus creating an emotional block; it is as if in that moment, that is when the bad event occurs, he does not feel the suffering because he takes life as it comes.
It is as if wrapped in a black cloud, which as suddenly as it has arrived, so it goes away. Mustard's depression and mood swings, unlike Gentian's, do not come from a specific cause. Mood changes quickly for no reason and often despite having everything you want you don't feel happy. Mustard characters often suffer a sense of malaise and psychophysical exhaustion, failing to react; in fact, there are cases in which these individuals have insomnia, inappetence, sexual disorders such as the total absence of sexual desire, menstrual pain in women, obsessive-compulsive personality disorders and mental confusion. With Mustard the values of serenity are rediscovered and changes are accepted with the certainty of reaching the goal. The flower remedy acts immediately, the person regains serenity and then fails to give an explanation of what happened. Mustard is magical for me, it makes you find happiness in little forgotten things like a walk by the lake, being in the sun, taking care of plants, animals; it makes the person serene and makes him forget power, possessions and fame, capable only of distancing from the meaning of life. Mustard is also very helpful in premenstrual mood swings.
Mustard-related moods and symptoms in order of importance:
- endogenous depression
- Causeless sadness
- Depression that comes and goes for no reason
- Depression of unknown cause

- Meloncholy
- Menses with instability
- Sudden change of mood

Definition of E. Bach

Those who are subject to periods of sadness or even despair, as if a cold and dark cloud overshadowed them, hiding from them the light and joy of life.
It may not be possible to give any reasons or explanations for such attacks. Such conditions make it nearly impossible to appear happy or cheerful.

Oak

It belongs to the "Aid" category.

Who needs this flower is a person who leads a life full of duties, works for duty, eats nutritious things for duty, leads a married life for duty, plays sports for duty, takes care of the loved one for duty. The person with this nature has great willpower, accumulates a lot of stress without ever collapsing, has a lot of energy and tenacity as well as being determined.

You agree to take charge of everything, you never give up the fight. Everything is over your shoulders.

As the oak plant is robust and resistant so is the Oak person. Not only is the person strong but he tends to overestimate his ability by exaggerating and taking charge of everything without listening to his own needs. Oak's classic symptom is a headache or something else that occurs on Sundays or in any case on rest days.

The Oak person is very dependable, but has a downside which is a stubborn refusal to let go and rest, even when this need is obvious to everyone around her. Clinically, the disease is viewed by the Oaks as a failure and efforts to heal them are generally superficial. It has often been found in these individuals the manifestation of autoimmune pathologies with characteristics that lead to the chronicity of the disease itself, such as asthma crises, in cases in which one is forced to abandon the obligations undertaken, rheumatoid arthritis, cervical , otosclerosis and arteriosclerosis. The Remedy helps these people stay strong in adversity but not get crushed by fatigue by becoming wiser and learning to recognize when it's time to stop.

Oak-related moods and symptoms in order of importance:
- Minimize your problems
- Minimize your needs
- Exaggerated dedication
- Heroic attitude
- Exhaustion from overwork
- Despair without resignation

- Covered tiredness
- Annoyance for the disease that does not allow you to be efficient
- Sense of duty
- Rigidity

Definition of E. Bach

For those who struggle, they struggle hard to heal, or to fulfill the tasks of daily life. They never get tired of trying one thing after another, even when their case seems hopeless. They keep fighting. They are dissatisfied with themselves if the disease interferes with their duties or ability to help others. They are courageous people, they fight against great difficulties, without losing heart or sparing themselves.

Olives

It belongs to the "Aid" category.
Anyone who needs this flower is an exhausted person, without physical or mental energy, with every slightest effort he gets tired even with the most banal one, like brushing his teeth, combing his hair, getting dressed, reading a book, taking a walk, in short, everything becomes an insurmountable difficulty.
The person is absent and without desires, from time to time a light of desire to do comes on, but immediately loses hope because above all the physical energy fails.
Olive brings enough energy to recover all that can be recovered. Olive restores energy in an incredible way but I recommend that you also look into the Oak state because if you don't convert your Oak state back, Olive is useless. It is useful to note the difference between Olive and Hornbeam, the latter is, in fact, the remedy against mental fatigue that is felt even before the effort is made, while Olive is given to restore the necessary strength, confidence and energy to move forward. Olive is a real energy supplement, it is indicated for those who show pallor on the face, body heaviness, dry skin, due to lack of fluids, low and passive mood, they can also suffer from anemia, daytime insomnia, hunger crises, it is often used during post-illness convalescence.
Olive-related moods and symptoms in order of importance:
- Physical tiredness
- Need for sleep
- Exhaustion
- Deep asthenia
- Physical exhaustion
- Lack of energy
- Nausea with excessive tiredness
- Exhaustion

Definition of E. Bach

Those who have suffered a lot mentally or physically and are so tired and fatigued that they feel exhausted, unable to make the slightest effort.
Daily life for them is hard work, without pleasure.

Pine

It belongs to the category of "Assistants".
They are perfectionists and set very high goals which can lead them to work excessively and strive to do better, but when the effort becomes too much for the body, they feel guilty for the resulting illness because they feel they are failing in their duty towards others, towards one's job and towards family responsibilities. This guilt complex takes much joy out of their lives and causes discouragement, if not even despair. They may often feel guilty about trivial matters, but such thoughts fill their minds to the point where they continually ask for forgiveness. We don't accept compliments and praise because we think we are never good enough for our tasks. We tend to live on the margins and avoid being noticed too much because we are ashamed of feeling too humble. The floral remedy harmonizes feelings of guilt, gives inner peace. The person will no longer accuse himself so easily, he will begin to rejoice in the results achieved in any project of his life because he will know how to accept recognition, he will devote himself more to himself and he will understand that there are also his desires to be satisfied. With Pine you love yourself for your potential, forgiving yourself and implementing a deep compassion for yourself and for the human being.
Pine-related moods and symptoms in order of importance:
- Inferiority out of guilt
- Regret with guilt
- Guilt
- Self-accusation
- Excessive gratitude
- Feeling of guilty conscience
- Anger towards oneself

Dr. Bach said that this feeling of guilt and self-reproach is a waste of time, as past mistakes are just experiences that teach us not to repeat them again. Once a lesson is learned, it will guide us to serenely face the same experience in the future. The good thing about Pine is that he recognizes his mistakes, but doesn't waste time dwelling on them, because he has learned not to repeat them. These are those who wish to take responsibility and shoulder the burdens of others when it really helps, but with the wise awareness that this is not always the best way to help.

Definition of E. Bach

For those who blame themselves.
Even when they are successful they think they could have done better, and they are never satisfied with their efforts or results. They are tireless workers and suffer greatly from the mistakes they attribute to themselves.
Sometimes, when someone else makes a mistake, they take responsibility for it themselves.

Red Chestnut

It belongs to the category of "Assistants".
Who needs this flower is a person who cares excessively for loved ones. This worry or fear becomes chronic when the thought that something bad could happen to a loved one (child, husband, partner, colleague, animal) becomes fixed, this condition in the long run can cause insomnia.
This person constantly watches over their loved ones and their lives, trying to change it to their own taste and liking, unknowingly creating numerous problems and inconveniences. It would seem the classic flower of apprehensive parents, in fact it is, but not only for parents but for all those who are afraid that something will happen to their loved ones. The slightest delay or the slightest sneeze immediately puts you in a state of excessive agitation. It allows you to break the umbilical cord that binds us to people or situations. The Remedy helps people who find themselves in this state of mind to think of their loved ones in a serene and calm way, so that, instead of communicating anxiety, they are of comfort and help. With Red Chestnut you live a free and safe life, you develop a great helping force towards others. Red Chestnut unlike Rock Rose, goes to act on a fear for others that never enters full terror, but which often creates an obstacle to healing.
The types of people that can be treated with this flower frequently suffer from nervousness or chronic fatigue, headaches and asthma, hypertension and addictions to nicotine food. Also worth mentioning is the fact that Dr. Edward Bach sometimes advised this flower not only to those who needed it, but also to those who were close to him; in fact, for example, it is recommended to a mother who is very apprehensive about her child or when there are close relationships of dependence between individuals, as well as in the weaning phase between mother and child.
Red Chestnut-related moods and symptoms in order of importance:
- Anxiety for loved ones

- Anxiety about the difficulties of others
- Negative thoughts about the health of loved ones
- Symbiosis umbilical cord to untie
- Anxiety for loved ones
- Limit the freedom of others for his fears
- Possessiveness in affections

Definition of E. Bach

For those who find it difficult not to worry about other people. Many times they come to no longer worry about themselves, but they can suffer a lot for the people they care about, often expecting unpleasant things to happen to them.

Rock Rose

It belongs to the category of "Healers" and is the twelfth plant discovered by Dr. Edward Bach.

Who needs this flower is a person who is easily frightened, at the ringing of a telephone, a bell, the fall of a book, a bottle, the scream of a person, an animal, the siren of a ambulance, in the presence of the police. etc. Usually this person is not fearful, but over time the accumulation of various shocks begins to create real panic attacks.

The positive state of Rock Rose makes the individual strong and courageous, in the blocked state, despite the fact that the person knows how to behave in the face of an emergency, one gets blocked, the energies are blocked, one is afraid bordering on terror and does not can think and act usefully. The floral remedy acts immediately in dangerous situations, it is instantaneous, it blocks terror and does not make you lose control. Rock Rose gives energy and restores a correct nervous balance even after particularly stressful events. Very useful in sudden anxiety attacks. With Rock Rose, safety and courage allow you to take any initiative, even in rescue situations. Rock Rose unlike Star of Bethlehem, which is used for past shocks, is used for recent, almost immediate traumas, in extreme cases moistening the lips with the remedy; the individuals here are gripped by fears that generate cold sweats, tachycardia, phobias, sudden anguish, heart pounding and shortness of breath.

Rock Rose related moods and symptoms in order of importance:
- Heart that seems to stop for fear
- Anxiety that blocks us
- Fear that blocks
- Fear after nightmares
- Loquacity for panic and distress
- Anxiety that makes you sweat
- Heart with accelerated rhythm for anguish
- Anxiety with tachycardia
- Terror of death
- Afraid that you do not want to admit

Definition of E. Bach

The emergency remedy for even seemingly hopeless cases. For accidents or sudden illness, or when the patient is very frightened or terrified, or if the condition is severe enough to cause great fear in those nearby. If the patient is unconscious, his lips can be moistened with the remedy.
Other remedies may also be needed in addition, for example, Clematis in case of unconsciousness, which is a state of deep sleep; Agrimony, if there is torment and so on.

Rock Water

It belongs to the "Aid" category.

Rock water is not a plant, but it is mountain water, rock water from Wales, England. It is born and gushes out in the middle of the rock and for this reason it is cold, rigid, but pure. Even today you can find small springs, with therapeutic properties, hidden among the vegetation, still uncontaminated places and subject only to the rules of nature: sun and wind.

Whoever needs this remedy is a very strict person in his way of life, he denies himself many entertainments and pleasures of life, respecting hard and rigid rules. Above all, she thinks about her health, she wants to be strong, active, and does everything to stay that way, she wants to be a good example for others. He is the fanatic of himself, he does not indulge in pleasures and adheres to his ideals with strength, determination and above all rigidity. Unlike the fanatic who wants to convince others (Vervain), Rock Water claims to be perfect and an example for others. Sometimes this mental rigidity has its physical counterparts. The ideals of reference can be different and range from sport, to nutrition, to work. The Rock Water remedy doesn't stop people from having high ideals and trying to reach them, but it helps to limit excesses, have more flexibility and not be so intransigent with themselves. Rock Water is the only Bach remedy that is not a flower, but pure spring water. This remedy, which often embodies the rigid feeling of those who undertake "strict" diets, together with Crab Apple, a purifying flower, is indicated to cure eating disorders such as anorexia.

With Rock Water life becomes adaptation, one's conceptions and ideals are lived with freedom and kindness.

Rock Water related moods and symptoms in order of importance:

- Pride that makes us masters of ourselves
- Need for perfection
- Inflexible with themselves
- Severity towards yourself
- Perfection is sought

- dogmatic idealism
- Self-satisfaction

Definition of E. Bach

Those who are very strict in their way of life; they deny themselves many joys and pleasures in life because they feel they might interfere with their work.
They are strict masters of themselves. They want to keep themselves healthy, strong, and active, and they do whatever they deem necessary to that end. Hoping to set an example for others who could then follow their ideas and ultimately become better.

Scleranthus

It belongs to the category of "Healers" and is the ninth plant discovered by Dr. Edward Bach.

Who needs this flower is a person who can't make a decision between two things, when it seems to her that one is right, immediately afterwards she thinks the other is right. This person is always indecisive and is his inner torment, but he never talks about it with anyone.

Mood changes easily from happy to sad. Faced with the need to choose between two options, one goes into crisis trying to evaluate the pros and cons of each possibility with the risk of getting bogged down in a dead-end road and with the risk of not trusting one's intuition. Scleranthus is very useful in balance problems such as carsickness and seasickness.

With Scleranthus the balance and clarity of one's choices are the basis of existence. The remedy is used to help the person act more decisively and understand what they really want. Diseases related to the Scleranthus type have been found such as dizziness, motion sickness, irritable bowel. Also, an interesting comparison is highlighted between the Cerato type, who always asks for the opinion of others and the Scleranthus person who never asks anyone for advice and tends to keep his dilemma all to himself, frequently generating symptoms with widespread malaise of various gender, from apathy, to depression, to difficult pregnancies.

Scleranthus related moods and symptoms in order of importance:

- Oscillating balance
- Unreliable due to uncertainty
- Alternation of activity and tiredness
- Mood alternation
- Apathy and hyperactivity
- Depression alternating with mania
- Uncertainty that no one confides in
- Nausea
- Instability during menstruation

- Bulimia alternating with anorexia

Definition of E. Bach

Those who suffer a lot because they can't choose between two things, because now one seems right now the other. They are generally quiet people and bear their difficulty alone, as they are not inclined to discuss it with others.

Star of Bethlehem

It belongs to the category of "Assistants".
Who needs this flower is a person who has received a shock: bad news, an accident, a bereavement, a disappointment, a trauma, a wound on the body, great frights, in short, an event for which the person is left without breath, as if frozen; in that precise moment she doesn't feel any reactions, she remains petrified.
Star of Bethlehem is one of the remedies that make up the Rescue Remedy. It is the remedy for any kind of shock, such as unexpected bad news or an unwanted and unexpected event. It can also be used for the effects of a shock many years ago, sometimes even the earliest in childhood. This remedy is also used for the sense of emptiness and loss that is sometimes felt when a loved one dies or moves away, as shock can be associated with these events. Star of Bethlehem is the Remedy that gives comfort in such circumstances. Useful for mourning or traumatic situations, small or large, but which do not allow a free flow of one's energy. It is a flower suitable for psychosomatic illnesses, for an asthma attack caused by stress, for insomnia, for amenorrhea and hysterical pregnancies, often these subjects also show strong disturbances such as sore throat due to tension.
With Star of Bethlehem, the necessary vital force is found, traumas are overcome and one feels one's soul consoled.
Star of Bethlehem related moods and symptoms in order of importance:
- Trauma
- Traumas of the past to dissolve
- You remain attached to a pain
- Depression as mourning
- Difficulty integrating events
- Refusal of consolation
- Shock
- Vital energies blocked

Definition of E. Bach

For those who suffer greatly under conditions which, for a time, cause great unhappiness.
The shock following bad news, the loss of a loved one, the fright after an accident, etc. To those who for a time refuse to be consoled, this remedy brings comfort.

Sweet Chestnut

It belongs to the category of "Assistants".
Who needs this flower is a person who finds himself experiencing a problem called "the sense of despair".
He believes he can solve every problem on his own with his own physical and mental strength and wants to prove it, and if fate holds bad surprises for him, he is convinced he can get out of it without asking for help. It is a devastating state of mind, as a result of which there is a collapse of both physical and psychological energy. You live in a state of total abandonment. The sensation is that of living inside a dead-end tunnel. This state of defeat is easily hidden from others, it can often be understood by the person's empty and resigned expression.
The remedy helps people suffering from this extreme state of mind to remain in control of their lives and to regain strength and hope. Sometimes a way out can open even at such a stage of life.
With Sweet Chestnut you live in the hope and certainty of a better life. You find your faith.
Moods and symptoms related to Sweet Chestnut in order of importance:
- Deep sense of isolation
- Complete resignation
- Extreme anxiety
- Total isolation, deep abandonment
- Deep anguish, desolation
- Anxiety as anguish
- Anxiety as desolation

Definition of E. Bach

For those moments that happen to certain people in which the anguish is so great as to seem unbearable.
When the mind or body feels they have reached their limit of endurance, and that it is time to give way. When it seems there is nothing left but destruction and annihilation to face.

Vervain

It belongs to the category of "Healers" and is the sixth plant discovered by Dr. Edward Bach in 1930.

Who needs this flower is a person who combines his psychic and physical forces to convince others of his ideas, his ideals, transforming himself into true missionaries, inflexible and intolerant. One is easily enthusiastic and absolutely wants to convince others of one's opinions as well. Injustices infuriate, taking sides. The fanatic, the enthusiastic driver, the champion of justice. Vervain has a constant need to feel alive by fighting battles and involving others in his missions. The excessive state of Vervain makes at times fanatical, hyperactive and tense. The remedy is given to help such people stop from time to time so that body and mind can regenerate. Vervain leads to stillness in taking pleasure in life and the passage of time instead of always feeling the need to be active.

With Vervain you live life with enthusiasm, with respect for others. You are a passionate inspirer and open to change. In hyperkinetic children this flower is used with success, it is also used in the treatment of headaches due to muscle and nervous tension, for fibromyalgia, muscle cramps and diarrhea. We can often use this flower together with Impatiens.

Vervain-related moods and symptoms in order of importance:
- Need to convince others
- You want to convince others
- Idealism and fanaticism
- You need to always be engaged in some battle
- Voltage
- Excessive self-esteem for which you think you are always right
- Aggression due to impulsivity
- Bulimia with voracity
- Hyperactivity

Definition of E. Bach

Those who have fixed principles and ideas, which they are convinced are right, and which very rarely change.
They have a great desire to convert everyone around them to their vision of life. They possess great willpower and much courage when they are convinced of those things they wish to teach. In sickness they continue to struggle long after many would have already given up on fulfilling their duties.

Comes

It belongs to the "Aid" category.

Who needs this flower is a person who wants to command everyone: he is a boss, a leader, a tyrant.

In life he can't stand being commanded but, on the contrary, loves to command; he is always in charge of something, of a company, of a team, of a group, of the family, he makes decisions for everyone because he is certain that he is doing their good.

Leader and dictator, what a huge difference. These two figures are the positive and negative representation of Vine. In the blocked phase Vine wants to convince others by dominating them, deciding for them. Vine people often have important roles in their work and in their interests and in the transformed state they can be excellent leaders by inciting and guiding others without forcing them and above all with respect for others. They are very different from Vervain-type people who instead try to convert others to their way of thinking, whereas Vine-types impose orders and discipline without admitting counteraction. The remedy develops this positive side of the Vine personality.

With Vine, one's authority is lived with confidence in oneself and in others. You also know how to delegate to others, thus also evaluating the potential of others. This remedy is used in many pathologies of musculoskeletal stiffness and arthritis, in fact it can be useful in cases of mental rigidity in people suffering from arteriosclerosis. It also includes the use of Vine in situations of heart attack and cardiovascular problems, neurovegetative disorders, halitosis and asthma and, in slightly bullying children, who are violent and overbearing and who beat up their schoolmates.

Vine-related moods and symptoms in order of importance:

- Inflexible with others
- Aggression to impose one's opinion
- Desire for command
- Tendency to dominate
- Authoritarianism by which you command

- Intransigence
- Uncertainty that makes you arrogant

Definition of E. Bach

Very capable people, certain of their ability, confident of success. Being so secure, they think it would be good for others if they could be persuaded to do things as they do, or as they are certain to be right. Even in sickness they give orders to those who assist them. They can be of great value in an emergency.

Walnut

It belongs to the category of "Assistants".
Whoever needs this flower is in a life-changing situation or is in a condition in which they do not have the strength to change, such as: marriage, divorce, new job, climate change, retirement, menopause, bereavement, pregnancy, vacation, new partner. Taking Walnut when experiencing a change facilitates adaptation by discovering new resources to easily experience the new situation.
It is also useful for those who are sensitive to the tensions of their surroundings and who tend to make them their own.
Also indicated for those suffering from meteoropathy (symptoms related to meteorological factors). Walnut helps break ties with the past, thus allowing you to continue on your path with confidence and without excessive suffering. With Walnut you are protected in changes, you feel safe and each new phase is lived with ease. In paediatrics, Walnut is indicated when children are experiencing a very specific stage of maturation or growth, as in the case of the child who has fixed teeth erupting and removes the milk ones, or it is used in puberty and adolescence to facilitate body change.
Walnut-related moods and symptoms in order of importance:
- To encourage any kind of change
- Menopause
- Hypersensitive to changes
- Stages of change
- Puberty
- Influenceable
- Teething
- Inconstancy

Definition of E. Bach

For those who have well-defined ideals and life ambitions which they are fulfilling, yet on rare occasions are tempted by the enthusiasm of others, convictions or strong opinions, to stray from their own ideas, goals, or work. The remedy gives constancy and offers protection from external influences.

Water Violet

It belongs to the category of "Healers" and was the tenth to be discovered by Dr. Edward Bach.
Who needs this flower is a person who has a lot of self-esteem, above the norm. She tends to be silent, calm, never lets herself be influenced by the opinion of others, often remains aloof, mysterious, dark, very reserved, haughty, willingly listens to other people's problems by giving advice. The problem with those with this nature is pride, it is difficult to apologize and if wrong, they have the ability to turn the situation around because they are convinced they are never wrong. However, we are responsible people who are appreciated and sought after by others, even if they are a little detached. "Home sweet home" is the motto of Water Violet. You feel safe in your environment, without too many jolts. This detachment from others can make you haughty or proud. Often their detachment is due to situations in which they could not express their emotional side. For this they close and stiffen.
The remedy can help bring them back into balance so that they can become more involved with others. Water Violets often suffer from eating disorders, hypertension, stomach aches, headaches. These characters are unable to express their feelings despite being their primary necessity; as a result, a small confrontation with Agrimony can be seen, he too hides his problems and is reluctant to express his true feelings, but for other reasons. In children, these characters are found in cases where they do not want to play and mix with others for pride.
With Water Violet you are wise and go through life with kindness and discretion.
Moods and symptoms related to Water Violet in order of importance:

- Pride and confidentiality
- Confidentiality and independence
- You want to solve problems yourself
- Stiff neck
- Individuality

- Joint stiffness
- There is little talk

Definition of E. Bach

For those who, in sickness or in health, like to be alone.
Very quiet people, who move without making noise, speak little and in a low voice. Very independent, capable and confident. They do not attach great importance to the opinions of others. They are secretive, leave people alone and go their own ways. Often sharp and talented. The calm and tranquility that distinguish them are a blessing to those around them.

White Chestnut

It belongs to the category of "Assistants".
Who needs this flower is a person who has totally lost control of the mind, lives in mental torment, thoughts are always the same and repeat themselves continuously without the will of the person. This state of mind can arise from various factors such as something that torments such as a phobia, a premonition, an intuition, a revenge, a disappointment. There are thoughts that keep coming back, even without wanting to. Problems become suffocating, as the mind always returns to them. Scratched record syndrome, yes, the old vinyl record that always came back on the same track. Well, with White Chestnut, thoughts and emotions always return to the same topics and facts, preventing us from seeing and implementing new solutions. The remedy is used to help people regain control of their thoughts in order to calmly and rationally deal with any issues that may be the underlying cause of their discomfort. White Chestnut is very useful in cases of insomnia, where you think over and over again about the same things, or when you can't relax during a sexual act because your head is somewhere else. In these characters it is easy to find cases of insomnia, in which one thinks over and over again about the same things and is unable to fall asleep, or when one is unable to relax during a sexual act because one's head is somewhere else. They may suffer from nervous tics, stress, tension headaches and anxiety disorders with obsessive-compulsive attitudes, sweating, dizziness. With White Chestnut the mind is calm and calmly finds every solution.
Moods and symptoms related to White Chestnut in order of importance:
- Lack of concentration from too many thoughts
- Persistent thoughts
- Circular thoughts
- Repetitive thoughts
- Mental confusion
- Continually ruminate on things to do

- Mental hyperactivity
- Insomnia from too many thoughts

Definition of E. Bach

For those who can't stop unwanted thoughts, ideas, arguments from creeping into their minds.
Generally during times when the interest of the moment does not have sufficient force to keep the mind occupied.
Thoughts that worry and don't go away, or if chased away for the moment, then they come back. They seem to go round and round and cause mental torture. The presence of such unpleasant thoughts displaces tranquility and interferes with the ability to think about daily work or pleasure.

Wild Oats

It belongs to the "Aid" category.

Who needs this flower is a person who never finds satisfaction in everything he thinks or does. He always has a thousand ideas to implement, many intuitions and in the end only indecisions, he continuously decides and even takes the initiative but while executing it he changes his mind again, project or other. His dissatisfaction can be seen in all its aspects. Indecision is generalized, not between two things. When choosing from a multitude of possibilities is difficult, Wild Oat helps you get your way. Classic example of the young person faced with the choice of the right school when all or many seem suitable. You would like to do something important but you don't know what. Wild Oat allows you to get in touch with your own skills and intuition.

The state of indecision of the Wild Oat type is different from that of the Scleranthus type, because in the second case the doubt is not about which direction to take, but rather about how to proceed or what to choose, despite having clear the various alternatives. Wild Oat people, on the other hand, don't know what the possible alternatives are because they haven't yet clearly defined their goals. The remedy helps these people understand what their true role is, making them rediscover their life purpose, so that they can clearly understand which direction to go. With Wild Oat you are able to do whatever you like, even if your interests are multiple, you know your destination. They often suffer from these characteristics of respiratory and hepato-biliary disturbances, irritable bowel, they are irritable subjects, with anemia, insomnia, often apathetic and sometimes anorexic with frequent sexual disturbances.

Wild Oat related moods and symptoms in order of importance:
- Lack of orientation
- Ambition without content
- Dissatisfaction
- Frequent job change due to dissatisfaction
- Illusions that do not allow you to take root

- Depression with resignation
- Excessive versatility
- dispersiveness

Definition of E. Bach

Those who have the ambition to achieve something important in life, who wish to have many experiences, to take pleasure in everything possible for them to live life to the fullest. Their difficulty lies in determining which occupation to follow; for although they have great ambitions, they have no particular vocation which attracts them above all others.
This can cause delay and dissatisfaction.

Wild Roses

It belongs to the category of "Assistants".
Whoever needs this flower is an apathetic, disinterested, listless, dull, anguished person, with no prospects, not alive, well. This state of mind can arise for various reasons or certain factors, such as for example: an incurable disease, a strong emotional disappointment, a strong shock, or, with the passing of life, when the person always leads the usual way of life. Routine makes you even more tired and listless.
You have no interest in your commitments and interests, you feel resigned with little energy. Even in the face of illness or a change, one doesn't have the strength to face them. The remedy awakens interest in life. The Wild Rose person in the positive phase will always be the happy-go-lucky type, but instead of being apathetic, they will feel that they have a purpose in life that will bring them greater joy and pleasure. Wild Rose offers the possibility to emerge from one's torpor with renewed enthusiasm. In these types there may be cases of emotionality and paranoid personality disorder, they are characters who often get sick with colds, flu, fever, sinusitis, allergies and eye problems including conjunctivitis. In children, they can be recognized in cases of excessive listlessness, recklessness to the point of hurting themselves, too long sleeps, with few movements.
With Wild Rose every moment is a source of joy, and one freely draws on one's inner strength.
Wild Rose related moods and symptoms in order of importance:
- Resignation without complaining
- Depression with apathy
- Apathy with indolence
- Apathetic resignation to events
- Apathy that does not allow you to do anything
- Apathy with resignation
- Apathetic sadness
- Depression with inner capitulation
- Crippling apathy

Definition of E. Bach

Those who, apparently, without sufficient reason, resign themselves to everything that happens, and let themselves slip through life, taking it as it comes, without the slightest effort to improve things and find some joy. They surrendered to the struggle of life without complaint.

Willow

It belongs to the category of "Assistants".

Whoever needs this flower is a person who has suffered an injustice, is embittered by some bad event that has happened or some project that has not been successful.

The person becomes suspicious and embittered, he thinks he has been wronged by life that he cannot overcome, but in doing so there are many reactions such as swallowing anger, harboring a sense of revenge, feeling bitterness, resentment, accumulating nervousness, all without ever be able to let off steam somehow. You don't feel sufficiently rewarded and loved by life, despite your efforts. It is thought that others have been more repaid for what they have done. The remedy encourages, instills confidence and optimism and helps the person in the negative emotional state Willow to be more generous in praising others and also more aware of how much her negative thinking can attract the very misfortune she blames on others.

With Willow you are the architects of your own fortune, you feel protected and helped in achieving the right merits. The remedy is indicated for those who suffer from love addiction which leads to envy towards the rich for example, mood disorders with a tendency to depression and sadness, which have consequences such as hair loss, psoriasis, wrinkles at a young age, appetite disturbances, neuralgia and chronic headaches. In addition, Willow is administered to grumpy, sulky and sulky children or to the daughter-in-law who has a grudge against her mother-in-law. Willow can be compared to Holly in that both are negative moods directed towards others. However, while the Holly persona burns with hatred and suspicion, Willow harbors resentment and self-pity.

Willow-related moods and symptoms in order of importance:

- Grudge with bitterness
- Self-pity because one feels like a victim of fate
- Feeling of injustice for trials they don't deserve to have to pass
- Bitterness because we consider ourselves unlucky

- Envy with resentment
- We feel like victims of adversity
- Bitterness causing lack of interest
- Bitterness with discouragement
- Lack of gratitude
- Inner bitterness
- Negativity
- Anger with a grudge

Definition of E. Bach

For those who have suffered adversity or misfortune and find it difficult to accept without complaint or resentment, as they judge life primarily in terms of success. They feel they didn't deserve such a great trial, that it was unfair, and they are saddened by it. They often have less interest and are less active in what they once enjoyed.

Rescue Remedy

By combining two or more flowers together, personalized blends can be obtained, i.e. aimed at a particular and subjective need. However, there is a combination prepared by Bach himself for general use; it is the emergency remedy called Rescue Remedy, a mixture of five flowers, which according to Bach would be useful in more acute situations: extreme stress, panic attacks, fainting, bad news, but also physical traumas. We can consider this "elixir" as the 39th flower, in reality it is a combination of 5 flowers that Dr. Edward Bach developed it in 1934, starting to use it as a means of therapeutic first aid in all emergency conditions, from physical trauma (for example a headache) to psychic one, and also from mourning, abandonment, loss , to the exams to be taken, to the postpartum. There are immediate benefits such as calm, serenity, relief, security, rebalancing of inner energies in stressful or particularly challenging situations. It also helps reduce fear and nervousness. As well as by mouth, this remedy can also be applied to the temples or wrists, or directly to the painful area.
It consists of a blend of:

- Star of Bethlehem, against sudden shock. As the acid that contains its flower, if touched, makes you cry, so the remedy helps to release a repressed emotion or any kind of trauma. It helps those who feel grief for a pain that comes suddenly (bad news, job loss, illness, bereavement, accident) or for the inconsolable loss of loved ones.

- Rock Rose, against panic or terror. Its characteristic thorns mean that if a person comes into contact with the plant, they are paralyzed by pain, especially if they injure their legs, which prevents them from walking. In the same way, the flower is used for paralyzing panic attacks, for external and internal trembling, sweating, tachycardia and blocking of the ability to react in an emergency situation. The flower helps those who let themselves be overwhelmed by their emotions, when fear turns into extreme panic and one gets stuck, with shortness of breath and heart in the throat, unable to react. In Rescue Remedy it is used for maximum anguish, to deal with a strong and acute state of terror or fear triggered by a traumatic event, accident or sudden illness.

• Impatiens, to restore calm. It is a plant that greedily absorbs water from the ground until the excess exudes from the leaves. As an indication of its constant activity, throughout the summer it bears shoots, flowers and seeds at the same time, without following the rhythms of the other plants. Its action in the Rescue Remedy serves to moderate impatience, anxiety from anticipation, excessive impetus, agitation, frustration or irritability towards a situation, which imposes a waiting time.

• Clematis, against the tendency to sag, the feeling of pulling away just before passing out. This climbing plant cannot take root in the ground because it has a very small root. Its guides hang down and give it a floating look. It is equally useful for people who cannot keep their feet on the ground, whose mind slips away from the present to fantasize about the future or alternative versions of the present. In Rescue Remedy it helps above all to avoid fainting and to alleviate that state of confusion and daze that can appear in emergency situations, when one would like to escape from reality.

• Cherry Plum, against the fear of losing control, of freaking out. Apparently calm, the plant is internally processing the flowers that will be born prematurely and in a compulsive way. The flower is for those who are afraid of going crazy, of acting irrationally, of making extreme and rash gestures, even self-harming, giving vent to dangerous impulses. He can't stop the sense of screeching noise of a thousand terrible thoughts that crowd into his head in a real mental overwork. He has the urge to commit violent acts that he is horrified by. In

Rescue Remedy it helps to regain calm, self-control and the ability to manage anger and all emotional states that can lead to violence.

It is the only remedy which, as a rule, is not prepared exclusively in liquid form, but also in lactose tablets and ointments. In the latter formulation, called "Rescue Cream" Crab Apple is added, the purification remedy, for its purifying effect; it can be useful on various occasions: traumas, small skin rashes, muscle pain and tension, dehydrated skin.
It is very useful, for example, in children, for small sudden fears, in cases of accidents, when receiving bad news (mourning, illness), sudden moments of anxiety, fears, panic attacks.
Put 4 drops of Rescue Remedy in a glass of water and sip it; initially with small sips close together (even every two or three minutes), then as the symptoms subside, the number of intakes is reduced. If you don't have the availability or don't have the time to take a glass of water, you can take 4 drops of the pure remedy. The Rescue is an emergency remedy, and should be used as such. It cannot replace the daily use of Bach flowers. To obtain good results and to be in good health with flower therapy, it is important to hire the most suitable flowers for each one, personalizing them on the basis of the current situation.